## Praise for the Creativ

Chuck Sutherland was blessec                                    ly
a unique work ethic but also a          ....  _..., couple
them with his own innovations, and turn them into concrete manifes-
tations that change not only the landscape but the lives of the people
involved. He believes that it is important to dream the dream but it is
equally important to be able to turn the dream into a reality. His book on
creative real estate financing is not from an instructor transmitting age-
old wisdoms to subsidized students. This book is about ideas that Chuck
has learned over the years, coupled with techniques he developed—ones
that have never been done by anyone else. The tracks are now laid for
those of you who read this book. He has led the way for those of you that
have the desire to build your dreams and ideas on top of his.

~Robert W. Steele, author of
*300 Ways to Buy, Sell or Exchange Real Estate*

Chuck Sutherland has provided answers to the exact issues I have as a
real estate investor, and I think most investors, new and seasoned have
as well—not only how to structure the financing, but the hands-on examples. They are invaluable. Most people just give vague ideas as if it is
top secret. Chuck has spelled it out! It makes me excited and challenged
to put these techniques into practice and to continue to test and grow
with them.

~Karri Speck, Real Estate Investor, Dallas, Texas

Chuck is telling you how it works in real life! It has been my privilege
to know and work with Chuck for many years in real estate and to attend many of the same marketing sessions. He is one of my first calls
when I need help structuring a transaction and have run out of ideas.

I have observed Chuck firsthand working through multi-property and multi-people transactions to find a way to help all parties get the set of "benefits" they need. This book is the clearest and most understandable presentation of creative financing strategies introduced I have ever read. The strategies are presented in the context of real-world scenarios where the core strategy can easily be understood and applied to multiple situations. Most important, the strategies presented are strategies that Chuck and his many professional colleagues in the "people-centered" segment of real estate use day in and day out. These strategies get transactions closed when traditional financing and transactions structures totally fail. This is a book you will want to keep close to your workspace if you ever do any real estate transaction.

~James T. Wilson, SEC, EMS

# CREATIVE SELLER FINANCING

## HOW TO USE SELLER FINANCING TO BUY OR SELL ANY REAL ESTATE

By: Chuck Sutherland

Published by Creative Real Estate Network
P.O. Box 110956, Carrollton, TX 75001
Chuck@CreativeRealEstateNetwork.com

First Creative Real Estate Network printing, September 2014
Second Creative Real Estate Network printing, June 2015
ISBN: 978-0-9964561-0-4

Find Chuck Sutherland online at CreativeRealEstateNetwork.com

# BOOKS BY CHUCK SUTHERLAND

Creative Seller Financing (2014)

Creative Down Payments (2015)

Advanced Creative Real Estate Financing (2016)

# DISCLAIMER

This book sets forth certain general approaches and techniques concerning seller financing of real estate. Neither the author nor the publisher are legal, tax, mortgage, title, or other professional experts. Furthermore, the author and publisher are not engaged in providing any of these services. The reader is advised to seek expert assistance concerning any of these or other real estate issues.

The names and locations of many of the parties in these real estate transaction examples have been changed, simply out of respect for their privacy. The prices, loan amounts, exact closing costs, and loan balances have also been changed—both to protect that privacy as well as to have the structure of the examples be simple and relevant. In some cases, the examples are consolidations of the specifics of several similar transactions.

Every effort has been made to make sure that all parts of this book are accurate. The reader should use this book only as a general guide and not as the authority on any particular area. The author and publisher shall not have any liability or responsibility to any person or entity for the use or misuse of any material in this book.

# DEDICATION

I dedicate this book to the pioneers of creative real estate techniques, in gratitude for what those techniques make possible for people.

# ACKNOWLEDGEMENTS

I acknowledge the following past and present members of the *Society of Exchange Counselors* who have contributed their knowledge and experience to me over the years and those who contributed their real estate examples for use in this *Creative Real Estate Book Series*, including: Chet Allen, Marilee Anderson, Steve Barker, Dana Barnes, Betty Beachum, Ed Berlinski, Bill Biddle, Corey Bishop, Ted Blank, Ron Bowden, John Brennan, Bill Broadbent, Jim Brondino, Dee Brown, Sam Brown, Larry Browning, L.R. Burton, Steve Bushey, Sandy Campagna, Rosebud Caradec, C. Charles Chatham, Rick Clark, Kim Colin, David Cook, Phil Corso, Jack Cox, Jim Crowley, Joe Crowley, Dennis Crull, Jack Dale, Madge Davis, Mark DiFranco, Wes Dingler, Chris Dischinger, Don Dobroski, Jeff Drinkard, Don DuBeau, Ernie Eden, Bob Elder, Steve England, Jon England, Nick Esterline, Steve Eustis, Jim Farley, Steve Fithian, John Fitzgerald, Peter Fortunato, Monte Froehlich, Walter Futtrup, Bob Giniecki, Leo Goseland, Hank Haden, Paul Hakim, Ebby Halliday, Arthur Hamel, Jack Harper, Daryl Hillman, Chuck Howe, Charles Huggins, Jack Hunt, Rex Jacobsma, Dick Janson, Wayne Jensen, Mark Johnson, Wayne Johnson, Will Jones, George Jonilonis, Jim Keller, Harry Kennerk, Ed Killian, Mike Lane, Tom Langel, Darrell Leason, Mark Lechner, Bill Macbeth, Paul Manza, Bill Martin, James Misco, Lance Moore, Roy Moore, Hal Morrison, Dan Murphy, Dan Murr, Marvin Naiman, Yvonne Nasch, Bryan Neal, Nick Nichols, Virgil Opfer, Tom Peterson, Hunter Quistgard, Marty Rader, Arthur Ramseur, Richard Reno, Bill Richert, Royce Ringsdorf, Ron Robinson, Danny Rosow, Alex Ruggieri, Brandon Sanders, Colby Sandlian, Richard Schindler, Jon Schweitzer, Arthur Scott, Margaret Sedenquist, Sheryl

Setzen, Jim Smalley, Jim Smith, Cindy Snell, Jon Spelman, Bob Steele, Steve Steffel, Rod Stewart, Bill Stonaker, Cliff Strand, Debbie Sullivan, Don Tardy, John Tyler, Gary Vandenberg, Ken Vidar, Lance Warner, Bill Warr, Clifford Weaver, Andy Wells, Peter West, Jim Wilson, Paul Winger, Paul Winger, Jr., Vicki Yeomans, Bob Zink, and others.

I also acknowledge those who, in some way, have directly contributed to the editing of this first book in the *Creative Real Estate Book Series*, including my wife Marilyn Sutherland, Kristen Eckstein (and her crew), Carolyn Weiss, Karri Speck, Julia Kappel, John Godbey, and Susan Bowman.

# Contents

# WHO IS CHUCK SUTHERLAND?

Chuck Sutherland is a national real estate developer, consultant, and speaker. He has been engaged in the creative real estate field for more than forty years. During that time, Chuck has both worked with and learned from some of the most creative real estate professionals in North America to make transactions in almost any circumstance.

Chuck Sutherland's *Creative Real Estate Seminars* are in high demand among buyers, sellers, and real estate agents seeking new approaches to making real estate deals. He brings creative ideas for potential deals, working with others to make real estate deals, developing properties, and turning around properties for added value.

In 2010, Chuck shared the *Society of Exchange Counselors* award for the "Most Creative Transaction of the Year." The transaction involved the exchange of fifteen different properties in five states among four different parties. In this transaction, he effectively demonstrated that a properly crafted deal with outstanding benefits for every party is almost impossible to be pulled apart by circumstances.

In this series of books on creative real estate, Chuck intends to help you gain the knowledge and ideas that you can use to make more and better real estate transactions to benefit yourself and others. If you would like to increase your knowledge of creative real estate further, check out Chuck's books at ChuckSutherlandOnAmazon.com and go to the CreativeRealEstateNetwork.com.

# A FREE GIFT FOR READING THIS BOOK

As a token of our appreciation for your reading this book, we are offering you a free gift:

a *Free Creative Seller Financing Checklist* for you to use in applying Creative Seller Financing to everyday real estate transactions.

Simply go to:

*http://CreativeRealEstateNetwork.com/freegift1*

to sign up for the Free Creative Seller Financing Checklist.

This Free Checklist is just one of the many benefits of the *Creative Real Estate Book Series.*

I wish you positive results in your real estate future!

Chuck Sutherland

# THE CREATIVE REAL ESTATE BOOK SERIES

You want to buy, sell, or finance properties. You may have many opportunities and ideas for doing real estate deals. And you may be constantly battling one of the biggest issues: "Where do I find the money to do a deal and/or where do my buyers or my sellers get the financing to close the deal?"

Financing, or the lack of financing, seems to always be in the way of closing the deals that you want, or need, to close. "But what can I do?" you ask. "I can't control the financing market!"

Well, maybe you can IF you are in the amazing world of creative real estate financing."

That is what this book on creative seller financing and the entire *Creative Real Estate Book Series* is all about: the creative art and science of obtaining or furnishing money or capital to buy real estate.

Use creative real estate financing strategies to make and close your deals!

## TRADITIONAL REAL ESTATE FINANCING

Traditional real estate financing is simple. As a buyer, you go to a financial institution (such as a bank) and borrow part of the purchase price, invest your money (or money you borrowed from another lender) to cover whatever balance is necessary, and buy a property. As a seller, you wait for the *perfect* buyer to make the *perfect* offer, and then negotiate and *possibly* agree on a *less-than-perfect* contract. Sometimes, using traditional financing works to close the transaction; sometimes it does not work at all!

There are numerous reference books and websites available on traditional real estate financing. They all detail the same traditional sources of financing real estate: banks and other financial institutions and guaranteed or direct loans via FHA, VA, HUD, and SBA. Sometimes traditional financing is easily available; other times, it is tight.

And, many times, traditional real estate financing offers the most benefits to the buyer and the seller, but not always. Frequently, you have to get creative in order to maximize the benefits for all parties and, most importantly, close the transaction at all.

## WHAT IS CREATIVE REAL ESTATE FINANCING?

Creative real estate transactions have been around since the first homesteader traded chickens to the banker for a mortgage payment. For example, the original city hall for Royse City, Texas, was the result of the city agreeing to build a two-story building and give the second story to the landowner in exchange for the land.

Creative real estate financing is a particular genre of financing real estate transactions. You could say creative financing is "outside the box" of traditional real estate financing.

But that simplistic definition obscures the rich possibilities and benefits possible to those who employ creative real estate financing strategies. You can take these strategies and create a completely new way of working with real estate.

The financing strategies in this book and the other books in the *Creative Real Estate Book Series* do not constitute all of the creative real estate financing strategies that you can use in a real estate transaction, as there are literally hundreds. But they are a representative sample of what is possible. They will get you started on the road to finding creative ways to finance any transaction.

## How to Get the Most from This Book

Included in this book are creative financing strategies involving houses, land, commercial properties, and investment properties as examples. Many of these strategies can work in both good economic times and challenging economic times.

The examples are designed to demonstrate how these strategies apply to all types of real estate. If you find that the example does not relate to the type of property you are interested in, use your imagination and examine how it could apply to your interests.

The material presented goes beyond the traditional financing sources and methodologies. I present materials that typical investors never learn. If knowledge is power, the material included here will indeed provide you with a great deal of power. But real power is power in action. I encourage you to "get into action" and explore the application of this material to your real estate situations.

Do not finish this book with a bunch of ideas that are just that—ideas or theories. I am asking you to put yourself into the picture. Imagine you dealing with the situations given in each example. Imagine how you could handle it. Imagine using the strategy yourself—wrestling to solve real problems and finding real, workable solutions to those problems. Put yourself in all the roles of the described situations and examples. You never know. From one transaction to the next, you may find yourself as the buyer, the seller, the lender, the borrower, the broker, or even some other role.

If you put the ideas in this book into action, then whether you read this book once or revisit it countless times, you will be gaining "practice" in solving these kinds of problems in your own life, in your own transactions. You will also make money!

# FUNDAMENTAL PRINCIPLES OF CREATIVE REAL ESTATE

## PRINCIPLE NO. 1: EMBRACE PROBLEMS AND CREATE SOLUTIONS

Problems are good! Webster's New World Collegiate Dictionary defines a problem as "a question proposed for solution or consideration." That is it! A problem is simply a question to be resolved.

You want to be looking for problems to resolve, but not just any kind of "problems."

You want to be looking for "people problems." After all, it is people who have problems. A building has no problems, even if it is falling down. The building doesn't care. But the owner might care; the lender might care; the neighbors might care; the tenants might care. Property problems are actually "people problems."

A solution is also defined by Webster's New World Collegiate Dictionary as "an answer to a problem." Now, we make the case that there are many possible answers to a problem, not just one. We assert that a solution is "one of many possible answers to a problem." By exploring this book you will see that there is an infinite variety of strategies to solve problems and close your transactions. In many cases, you could apply several of these strategies and close the deal—you just have to structure the solution so it is a win for everyone.

Open your own mind to possible solutions for the people problems beyond the conventional thinking. After all, this book is about "creative" real estate financing, not "the ordinary and usual" real estate financing.

By the way, when you ask people what problems they are dealing with in buying or selling a property, you will find that the initial problem people describe is usually not the real problem. People who need to sell a warehouse or house for cash could want it to pay for a child's college, buy a home near family in another city, pay down debt or a tax bill, or buy a vacation home. The problem is not just that they need cash. They are trying to resolve a problem in their life. What's the real problem? You cannot find out unless you use the principle of "getting all of the facts."

## PRINCIPLE NO. 2: GET ALL OF THE FACTS

What do I mean by "facts"? I define facts simply as "the state of things as they are."

Yet, when you really look at it, most of us are far less concerned with the facts than with our opinions about the facts. We want to agree or disagree with whether someone should or should not have done something. "They were wrong" or "You were robbed" or "They are so unfair in their lending policies." These are all opinions—not facts.

To solve a problem, you must start with the factual details of the situation: the property, zoning, the owner, the lenders, the neighbors, the community, building setbacks, and everything else that is pertinent. The more relevant the facts you can gather, the greater the chance you have of understanding the situation you are dealing with.

Getting the facts about the people issues requires asking questions—questions that allow people to talk freely about themselves and the issues with which they are dealing. Ask open-ended questions that elicit something more than a "yes" or "no" answer. In that way, you will learn far more than the question you are asking. Remember from principle of embracing problems and creating solutions that you need to understand the people problems. To understand them, you must ask and listen.

Use questions that others are unwilling or afraid to ask, like: "What are your plans after you sell this property?" or "What is the current situation on your mortgage?" or "To what extent have you gone over your tax situation with your CPA?" You can ask these otherwise intrusive questions in an unobtrusive way. Simply tell the truth. tell the other parties that there are certain things you need to understand to reach an agreement that will work for all parties.

From these questions, you gather the raw material to determine the problems to be resolved and formulate possible solutions. You have a more solid foundation from which you can support your situation, and can now work towards putting together a deal that works. Ultimately, the people you ask will appreciate that you asked these questions, because you will help them understand and achieve what they truly want.

## PRINCIPLE NO. 3: WORK WITH MOTIVATED PEOPLE

It is usually more profitable to work with a buyer or seller who *really* wants to or needs to do a transaction. A motivated buyer, seller, or lender will *do* more to get the deal done than an unreasonable party who wants to win at the expense of others in the deal or someone who is unmotivated. The test of a motivated person in a deal is in finding out what they will *do*.

Be relentless in discovering what people will "do" in order to uncover how best to put together a deal. Will a seller provide—or at least consider—seller financing? Will he or she accept other real estate as a down payment? Would this seller consider leasing part of the property back after closing?

You will never put together a deal with someone who is not motivated to make the deal. I would rather work with someone who is broke but highly motivated than with a multimillionaire who has no motivation to really close a transaction. Cut your losses when you discover there is insufficient motivation to make a deal; redirect your efforts to people who are truly motivated to solve a problem.

## PRINCIPLE NO. 4: CREATE NET BENEFITS FOR EVERYONE INVOLVED

Many books on real estate assume that one party will be attempting to take advantage of another party. When you believe that and act on that assumption, it usually results in transactions where you trick someone into doing a deal or work hard to avoid being tricked (so the deal probably does not close). Either you take advantage of another person's misery and stress or you fear they will take advantage of you.

That kind of deal can easily fall apart given that the only thing holding it together is the stress and misery of the other party.

But there is another way.

The way is have everyone in the deal win. Create transactions where the buyer and seller can be of service to one another. However naïve you might at first think it sounds, there is a way where everybody wins!

Now, an "everybody wins" scenario does not mean that all parties will be completely thrilled or enthusiastic about the transaction that they are making. You are not looking to make the other parties happy in a transaction. Making people happy is a futile pursuit. But it is in your best interest that the others involved are satisfied with the transaction. People will do a transaction because of the net benefits that they receive in the transaction.

A benefit could be defined as an advantage or profit gained from something and a detriment could be defined as a disadvantage or loss from something. Only if all of the perceived benefits for each party are greater than the perceived detriments for each party will a transaction actually be completed. Detriments, like benefits, are completely individual to each party and each situation. What looks like a detriment to one party may be a non-issue or even a benefit for another party.

Net benefits can be *constructed* so there is enough to go around for everybody (I win/you win)`. In the end, there have to be more benefits/positives than detriments/negatives, or the deal will not close. Those net benefits are also the reason that others in the transaction will work with you in the future.

## Principle No. 5: It's about the People, Not Just the Property

To do creative deal making, you must create a relationship with the other players. If you are a buyer, you must create a relationship with the seller. If you are the seller, you must create a relationship with the buyer. It takes courage for people to think outside the box. If they do not feel that you care about them at all, they will be unwilling to think and act outside the box, and nothing will change. Relationship is the foundation—without it, you cannot build a deal that will work.

## Principle No. 6: Employ Qualified Professionals

By employing professionals, you not only protect yourself from mistakes, but you also gain the confidence to take action where you might otherwise hesitate or freeze.

Be sure to obtain qualified legal counsel in any real estate or financing transaction. Remember that all attorneys are not created equal. Find a knowledgeable real estate attorney who will represent your legal interests and keep you out of trouble without making your business decisions for you. Also, make sure you choose an attorney with whom you can effectively work.

For example, these creative real estate transactions are not traditional, so an attorney who only thinks inside the box may have difficulty with some or all of these transactions. These strategies are legal, but they are uncommon – so you need to work with someone who can think beyond traditional transactions.

There are also complex tax implications in any real estate transaction. In that respect, creative real estate transactions are no different from traditional transactions. Get a qualified CPA to advise you on the tax implications of any real estate transaction you are contemplating. And, like attorneys, CPAs come in all flavors. Find one with whom you can work and who will advise you well. Solicit their advice often, especially when you venture into new territory.

Title companies are critical to the success of any transaction, particularly when they provide closing services. In some states, attorneys fill this role. In other states, real estate brokers can close transactions. Regardless, you want to find a closing agent that you can count on for both responsiveness and open-mindedness. The open-mindedness is critical as you negotiate real estate and financing strategies that are nontraditional. Select a title company or closing agent who has experience closing complex transactions. Work with them consistently. Train them. Be loyal.

Many real estate brokers either do not understand or are not interested in creative approaches. Find a broker in your local area who is knowledgeable and who has high integrity. This person can teach you a lot about the local market and, perhaps, you can teach this person a thing or two as well.

In summary, work with professionals who are knowledgeable and skilled, and pick the ones with whom you work best. It may take time to find the right people, but it is worth it. These are the key creative real estate principles.

## STRATEGIES, NOT FULL SOLUTIONS

All of these principles are strategies to use, but they are not full solutions by themselves. You have to apply the strategy to the particular people and circumstances of the transaction. The *application* of any strategy in a particular situation can make the difference between big profits or big losses and lots of aggravation. Use good business principles in managing the details of the transaction. Get good advice.

For example, if you are renting a house and your tenants miss several payments, you are losing money and they are living for free—unless your contract gives you the ability to evict them quickly. If you did not put in a clause in your contract for late fees, they may pay late every month. If you need their payment to pay your loan on this or another investment, and your cash flow is tight, you yourself may be at risk of foreclosure.

If the strategy here is "renting a house to get monthly income," depending on how this plays out and what your contract says, you could have a non-paying tenant that you can evict within a few months or a non-paying tenant that you cannot evict. Your contract reflects how you actually apply the strategy.

This is why you need a professional. If you are not a seasoned investor or real estate broker or real estate tax expert, I hope by now you are clear you need to involve one or more of these experts in working with you.

It is worth the extra eyes on your contract to be sure that, as part of creating net benefits, you win as well as the other party. Even if you are a seasoned investor, subtle changes in the deal could put you at risk in the deal in unexpected ways. It is best to work with your qualified and experienced advisors every time

In this book, we have not spent time dealing with the history of financing since the Napoleonic era, or the philosophical examination of the intrinsic nature of financing, or even my personal opinions about financing in the various parts of the world. This is a book about "real deal" creative financing techniques. It is designed to give you tools you will not find anywhere else: creative tools to close deals when regular financing cannot.

My intention is to give you as much meat as possible for your discovery of these techniques for yourself.

## The Names Have Been Changed

Either I or someone I personally know has employed every strategy in this book and in the entire Creative Real Estate Book Series. I have changed the names and locations of many of the parties in these real estate transaction examples simply out of respect for their privacy. I have also changed prices, loan amounts, exact closing costs, and loan balances—both to protect that privacy as well as to create examples that are simple and relevant in structure. In some cases, the examples are consolidations of the specifics of several similar transactions.

Regardless, these strategies have been field tested over many years by many different people. They work! Like everything else in life that works, however, these strategies must be employed in the appropriate situation and executed in the correct manner. The strategies must also be applied within the standards of any particular state's laws and regulations.

## And Now It Is Time!

Now it is time to explore this rich world of creative real estate financing strategies.

Ready, set, go!

# INTRODUCTION TO CREATIVE SELLER FINANCING

In this book, you will learn many different styles of creative seller financing. Seller financing is when the seller of a property makes a loan for a buyer to purchase the seller's property. The outside-the-box application of seller financing is creative seller financing in action.

You will learn how to apply the different styles by walking step by step through examples of each type of seller financing. You will learn how to apply the different tools to both residential real estate and commercial or investment real estate. Understanding the tools will give you more facility in completing real estate transactions, resulting in expanded benefits to all parties involved. Said another way, creative seller financing will help you close more deals!

By the end of this book, you will be clear that you can do any of these types of transaction using creative seller financing!

There are many different ways to use the tool of seller financing in real estate transactions. The loan the seller gives to the buyer could be a first mortgage, a second mortgage, or a third mortgage. The loan could be secured or unsecured. The buyer could secure the loan with the property the seller is selling, or secure the loan with a completely different property.

We use the term creative financing as opposed to the term conventional financing. Conventional financing is normally originated, funded, or guaranteed by conventional lenders; banks, credit unions, mortgage bankers, Farm Home Administration (FHA), and the United States Department of Agriculture, among others. While creative financing sometime involves conventional financial institutions, the creative investor is the one who brings the unconventional thinking that makes all the difference to making the transaction.

Seller financing is one of the simplest methods of creatively solving a financing problem in the acquisition or sale of real estate. The seller simply finances all or part of the buyer's purchase price. This seller financing strategy can frequently make the down-payment requirements easier to afford or increase other benefits to the buyer.

In most cases, the seller providing the financing receives both a promissory note as evidence of the debt and a pledge of the real property as collateral for the repayment of the debt. The pledge of real estate as collateral is called a mortgage in many jurisdictions. It is also known as a deed of trust in some states and as a lien in other states. In this book, we will use the term "mortgage" to represent all the various forms of pledges of security for a loan.

The pledge may be in "first position" (such as a first mortgage or first deed of trust) or may be in a "second position" (such as a second mortgage or second deed of trust). I have even heard of situations where the mortgage is in fourth or fifth position.

Why would a seller make these kinds of transactions? Simple! It is because, in those situations, the solution provides more benefits to the seller than the other available alternatives. The key is to be able to determine or draw out what benefits are available to each party in the transaction from various seller financing scenarios.

How would you identify when seller financing may be viable as an option? Whether you are the buyer or the seller in a transaction, seller financing may offer higher benefits because of a variety of factors. For example:

## CREATIVE SELLING FINANCING

The seller may want to:

- Maximize the price on the sale

- Make a sale instead of losing a sale

- Sell a property in difficult markets

- Develop monthly net income at a higher interest rate than available elsewhere

- Preserve capital for retirement

- Own a note with payments secured by a known property

- Receive greater benefits because of his or her tax position

- Receive a monthly payment

The buyer may want to:

- Reduce the payments on the loan for a period of time

- Reduce the down payment required to buy the property

- Preserve capital

- Increase yield

- Solve problems in qualifying for a conventional loan

- Avoid the delay and procedures of qualification at a typical financial institution

- Obtain different terms on a loan than available from a typical financial institution

- Leverage the use of proceeds on property to be sold in the future

In many ways, seller financing is almost identical to institutional financing. The main difference is that the seller, who is now a private lender, is the one providing financing to the buyer instead of a financial institution. If the buyer defaults on the terms of the financing and the seller has the property as collateral for the repayment of the loan, the seller has all the options available to financial institutions. That includes everything from rights for collection of payments all the way to a suit of foreclosure to take possession of the property.

The individual owner of a seller-financed mortgage has one significant advantage over a typical financial institution: The owner of a seller-financed mortgage can actually negotiate one-on-one with the borrower. This is extremely useful in situations like negotiating new terms, changing interest rates, and dealing with unexpected breakdowns.

In the next chapter, we briefly examine the impact of recent legislation and regulations on seller financing in general. In the chapter titled "Basic Seller Financing," I will lay out the steps involved with a *basic* seller-financed transaction. It is the first step outside-the-box. In later chapters, I will examine other more creative seller financing options and show examples of their use. You can also always go to my website for additional information at *http://CreativeRealEstateNetwork.com*

# THE SAFE ACT AND THE DODD-FRANK ACT

You should be aware that seller financing is not as simple as it used to be. There are new restrictions imposed by enactment of both the Secure and Fair Enforcement for Mortgage Licensing Act of 2008 ("SAFE Act") and the Dodd-Frank Act. But there is "light at the end of the tunnel" as I will show in this chapter.

## THE SAFE ACT

The SAFE Act requires state-licensed mortgage loan originators (MLOs) to meet certain licensing, compliance, and underwriting requirements. Furthermore, the act requires that all state-licensed MLOs register with the Nationwide Mortgage Licensing System & Registry (NMLS). The individual states have enacted their own regulations to regulate mortgage lending to comply with the act.

One key thing to remember about the SAFE Act: anyone who engage in the activities of a loan originator" could be determined to be one. The SAFE Act defines an MLO as an individual who takes a residential mortgage application and offers or negotiates the terms for compensation. The Regulation Z rule defines "loan originator" slightly differently as a person who performs any of the following activities for compensation: takes an application; or offers, arranges, or assists a consumer in obtaining, applying, or negotiating an extension of consumer credit; or advertises that they'll perform the activities described above. (Source: http://news.cuna.org)

Those definition of a mortgage loan administrator leave owners vulnerable in providing seller-financing. Under the SAFE Act, there is exclusion for up to five seller-financed transactions in every 12-month period under certain criteria. A seller financing the sale of his or her own property could also completely avoid the issue of licensing by retaining the services of an independent licensed loan originator.

For the most part, the Nationwide Mortgage Licensing System & Registry and the state-enacted legislation which followed fulfills the original intent of the SAFE Act. Some of the restrictions the SAFE Act created have been superseded by the Dodd Frank Act, including the criteria for seller financing of residential properties. But the idea of an exclusion for seller financing under certain conditions still remains as a part of the Dodd-Frank Act as we will next discuss.

## THE DODD-FRANK WALL STREET REFORM AND CONSUMER PROTECTION ACT

The Dodd-Frank Wall Street Reform and Consumer Protection Act (Dodd-Frank) is a broad financial reform package affecting virtually every corner of the financial services industry. Since its inception, the act has come under continuing criticism, legal setbacks, calls for reform or outright repeal. The entire act is way beyond the scope of this chapter. We will focus only on the effect the act has on seller-financed, real estate transactions.

For the real estate market, Dodd-Frank provides that creditors wishing to make residential mortgage loans to owner-occupants must first determine that the borrowers have the ability to repay, based on specific statutory criteria:

current income or assets
current employment status
credit history
monthly mortgage payment

other monthly mortgage payments arising from the same purchase

monthly payment for other-mortgage-related expenses (e.g., property taxes)

the borrower's other debts

borrower's debt-to-income ratio

The act does not apply to commercial or investment real estate transactions. However, it does apply to "any residential dwelling that contains 1-4 units, including houses, apartments, townhouses, condominium units, cooperative units, mobile homes, and trailers or boats used as residences. The rules apply whether the individual is purchasing a primary residence, second home, or vacation residence." [From an article by Michael A. Smeenk entitled "Dodd-Frank, Consumer Financial Protection & Owner Financing" located at http://frascona.com ]

Additionally, an owner-financed note must have a fixed rate or, if adjustable, may adjust only after five or more years and be subject to reasonable annual and lifetime limitations on interest rate increases. Negative amortization loans (always risky) must be accompanied by disclosure and counseling for first-time buyers. And prepayment penalties are banned.

There exist two exclusions for sellers making sales to residential owner-occupants. The first exclusion is the "Three Properties Exclusion" where sellers who finance the purchase of three (3) or fewer properties in a 12-month period. The second exclusion is the "One-Property Exclusion" where the seller must be a "natural person" and can only finance the sale of a single property in any 12-month period. These are discussed in the following *Excerpt from the 2013 Loan Originator Rule Small Entity Compliance Guide issued by the Consumer Financial Protection Bureau*

# Excerpt from the 2013 Loan Originator Rule Small Entity Compliance Guide issued by the Consumer Financial Protection Bureau (pages 22-23)

### When is a seller financer a loan originator?

(§ 1026.36(a)(4) and (5)) Seller financers that engage in a minimum number of transactions are considered creditors under the Truth in Lending Act (TILA) and Regulation Z. Specifically, seller financers would be considered creditors under Regulation Z if they extend credit secured by a dwelling (other than high-cost mortgages subject to § 1026.32) six or more times in the preceding calendar year, or extend more than one high-cost mortgage in any 12-month period. Accordingly, such seller financers are excluded from the definition of loan originators for purposes of the compensation provisions unless they use table funding. In addition, the rule contains two additional special exclusions from the compensation, steering, qualification, and identification provisions for certain seller financers. These exceptions are:

1. You are a natural person, estate, or trust and you provide seller financing 1. for only one property in any 12-month period.

2. You are any type of seller financing entity and you finance the sales of three 2. or fewer properties in any 12-month period.

Specifically, under the first special exclusion, if you are a seller financer that is a natural person, estate, or trust, you are not a loan originator if:

- You provide seller financing for only one property in any 12-month period.

- You owned the property securing the financing.

- You did not construct, or act as a contractor for the construction of, a residence on the property in your ordinary course of business.

- The financing meets the requirements below.

The financing must:

- Have a repayment schedule that does not result in negative amortization.

- Have a fixed rate or an adjustable rate that resets after five or more years. These rate adjustments may be subject to reasonable annual and lifetime limits

If the financing agreement has an adjustable rate, you must determine the rate by adding a margin to an index rate. The index you use must be widely available, such as the U.S. Treasury securities indices or LIBOR.

Under the second special exclusion, if you are a seller financer (regardless of whether you are a natural person, estate, or trust), you are not a loan originator if:

- You provide seller financing for three or fewer properties in any 12-month period.

- You owned the properties securing the financings.

- You did not construct, or act as a contractor for the construction of, a residence on the property in your ordinary course of business.

- The financing meets the requirements below.

The financing must:

- Be fully amortizing.

- Have a fixed rate or an adjustable rate that resets after five or more years. These rate adjustments may be subject to reasonable annual and lifetime limits.

Further, you must determine in good faith that the consumer has a reasonable ability to repay the loan. If the financing agreement has an adjustable rate, you must determine the rate by adding a margin to an index rate. The index you use must be widely available, such as the U.S. Treasury securities indices or LIBOR.

## KEY POINTS

1. The Dodd-Frank Act does put some constraints upon seller-financing of residential properties. However, for most sellers this will not apply as long as they take care to follow the requirements for the exclusions.

2. For all of the above complexity of these regulations and transactions that are excluded from these regulations, I do recommend you work only with an attorney who is trained in the technicalities of owner-occupied seller financing and the exclusions under of the Dodd-Frank Act. (See the short advisory

on Finding Knowledgeable Legal Counsel by James T. Wilson that follows)

3. Even given those new restrictions, understanding the creative seller financing options discussed in this book will give you an opportunity to build your income and net worth, solve problems that are not easily resolved, and be free of the constraints imposed by conventional financing.

4. The real seller financing opportunity for real estate investors still exists under a number of scenarios:

   • Seller financing under one of the Dodd-Frank exclusions

   • Lease to tenant with an option to purchase

   • Investor buying from home owner using seller financing

   • Investor selling to other investor using seller financing

   • Plus: Other creative financing strategies, some of which are contained in this book and in our other books on creative real estate.

5. While there are new restrictions for seller financing under the SAFE Act and under Dodd-Frankly, there will always be people who want to own their own home no matter what! And creative real estate owners, buyers and investors will find new ways to help those people do just that. While the federal government changes some of the rules we operate under, those who creatively adapt will profit the most!

# FINDING KNOWLEDGEABLE LEGAL COUNSEL

By James T. Wilson

Asking friends and acquaintances is one way to identify "candidates" for legal counsel, but is often not a great source. Many people do not have the knowledge or expertise/experience to recognize competent legal counsel from an attorney they like. As with any area of advisory or any other service, we should be seeking a specialist in dealing with our specific area of need. In this case, a real estate attorney with current knowledge and experience in handling transactions with seller financing.

Today, we have Internet resources. Check the listings of attorneys in your area that specialize in real estate. Check multiple sites and lists. Many listings only include attorneys who pay a fee to be listed. Bar Associations often have online listings. Identify candidates and then go to their individual websites or maybe some social media sites for detailed information. Since the rules we are addressing are relatively new, any reference to real estate financing expertise on the individual website should get your attention. If the listings in your area, do not provide what appear to be good candidates, expand the geographic location to find an attorney. In this case, traveling a few mile or maybe many miles to get competent advice and services is a cheap price to prevent inadvertent violation of the rules and the penalties that come with such violations.

Another good resource is real estate investors groups and conferences. In many areas there are organizations with both websites and regular meetings. Check their websites and go to their meetings. Often, knowledgeable and experienced attorneys are sponsors or attendees at meetings. Such organization have members who are acquiring and selling multiple properties. Such active real estate investors and operators are a good source to identify the type of competent legal counsel needed. That is especially true of "house flipper." House flippers are particularly subject to the subject seller financing restrictions.

After identifying candidates, how do I know which ones are knowledgeable and competent. The first thing is to clearly understand that you are interviewing the attorney and not that the attorney is allowing you to be their client. Ask questions! Even if you have to buy 30 minutes or an hour from the attorney to discover their competence, it is less expensive than expensive problems in the future. What questions?

- "I am potentially going to be selling several properties in the future and want to carry seller financing for long-term income. I have read and heard that there are some new restrictions on seller financing. Could you explain those restrictions in layman's terms?" You know the overview of the restriction as presented above. If the attorney cannot provide an overview at least as complete as the overview in this article off the top of their head, they are probably not your attorney.

- I have heard that the restrictions are treated differently from state to state. How are the new restrictions being treated and enforced in this state?

- What volume of your transactions in the past year have included seller financing?

- How do you advise your real estate clients to monitor when they get close to being affected by the new regulations?

You can probably think of other questions that you need to have clearly answered so you can operate effectively. The key is that you need a competent, knowledgeable (up to date knowledge) and experienced legal counsel with whom you can work easily. Your need the best team you can assemble and competent legal counsel is critical.

Do not hesitate to ask the hard questions. If the attorney takes offense or becomes defensive, they are probably not your attorney. Remember it is your money and time that you are putting at risk when you do a transaction that might have some regulatory restrictions with penalties.

# BASIC SELLER FINANCING

## STRATEGY

Let's begin with the simplest type of seller financing, what I call "basic" seller financing. In such transactions, the terms of the seller-financed mortgage are similar to that offered in a traditional loan by an institutional lender. The typical terms of a traditional loan are:

- Conservative loan to value ratios (for example, a loan for 80% of value)

- Market interest rates: for example, a relatively low interest rate

- Long-term amortization of payments: for example, payoff of loan over thirty years

- Recorded security instruments: for example, mortgage is filed of record

The examples that follow show some minor variation from the basic terms. In reality, every seller-financed real estate transaction includes some degree of variation from the basic standards. That is because *real transactions* occur only in the context of the reality of the circumstances, aspirations, and needs of the parties to the transaction.

The examples in this section illustrate some degree of adherence to the traditional model. In the sections that follow, I will explore creative seller financing, which steps beyond the traditional to create increased benefits for all the parties involved.

Basic seller financing allows a buyer to create built-in financing and allows the seller to achieve the "must-haves" wanted in a sale. "Must-haves" are the net benefits—after everything is negotiated—that the buyer and seller must have to execute the contract and close the deal. Remember, what people say they must have and what they *really* must have to sign a contract can be completely different. If everyone who started out saying that cash is required actually followed through on that, there would be little need for creative seller financing.

As a strategy, the terms of seller financing can make or break the deal. Every term of the seller-financing strategy can be used to complete a successful transaction. For the buyer, those terms may include a lower down payment, lower interest rate, and lower payments (thereby increasing the cash flow if the buyer leases the property). As a buyer, you never really know what a seller will accept until you make a written offer.

The lesson then is to always make a written offer. The written offer also leads to a seller taking your offer more seriously. The seller sees the written offer as the first step toward getting a contract that will close.

Basic seller financing and the other strategies to follow frequently allow the seller to both get the desired price and to get the property sold quickly. This benefit can be particularly important for those sellers who need (or want) to be free of the obligations of ownership. These obligations include loan payments, taxes, maintenance, and management. The seller can also receive interest income from buyer's payments against the loan. Finally, the seller can eventually realize the full benefits from having owned the property.

What are the conditions that are best for seller financing?

- Seller does not need a chunk of cash from the sale—the seller can benefit from receiving monthly income, relief from the operating expenses, or other benefits by selling.

- Seller owns the property free and clear or has a smaller loan on the property so negotiations do not need to involve a bank or other financial institution.

- Buyer can afford the payments but just needs the down payment, and so is a reliable party to make the monthly payments to the seller.

- The market is likely to improve so that, if the buyer defaults on the contract, the seller will get the property back and the market will be better—meaning the seller could get a higher price or better terms.

The examples also show how basic seller financing allows a buyer and seller to close a transaction that might not otherwise close. Understanding basic seller financing is useful. The above examples demonstrate the concept, but you can be expand and apply the strategy to many different actual situations.

## Residential Example

A consulting client of mine named Linda wanted to buy houses as investment properties. She had a plan to accumulate fifty properties over five years. Quite an undertaking! However, Linda saw that owning rental property over the long term could really provide her with financial freedom and a specific level of monthly income. Seller financing was a key to helping her reach her financial goals.

The game plan was to acquire those houses with very small down payments and seller financing for the balance. She intended to hold the houses for the long term and let inflation do the rest.

If Linda could buy on the right "terms," she could even afford to pay higher prices than her competition. After all, many sellers were motivated to get their price.

Linda found a house for sale for $125,000. The house was in only fair condition and had been on the market for several months. Nonetheless, it was clearly worth the asking price even in the current condition. Potential owner-occupants were turned off by the condition of the house and "wholesale buyers" were looking for deep discounts in the price. Consequently, the seller had received no acceptable offers.

The seller needed to sell the house to accept a job in another city. While he was motivated, he had many complaints about how buyers would "beat him down" on the price. The seller had adamantly told Linda that he was unwilling to be "taken advantage of." He wanted his "asking price."

Every seller or buyer has their important must-haves where they absolutely must have a particular term in the sale. Whether the must-haves are based upon reality or not, they are very real to the people involved. Being able to recognize these requirements, which may be based on emotion, and incorporate them into the transaction to work for all parties is critical for making effective transactions.

In this case, the seller did own this house free and clear of all loans. A free and clear property meant that there were no third party lenders to deal with in negotiating the transaction. That got Linda's attention as she saw an opportunity to accomplish her goals while assisting the seller in accomplishing his goals.

## SOLUTION

Linda offered to buy the house for $125,000 with $5,000 down and a long-term seller-financed note for $120,000. The note would be payable at 3 percent annual interest and amortized over thirty years with a ten-year balloon payoff. Note that the price offered was full price! The seller was now close to realizing an important objective to him: getting his price (and not being "taken advantage of").

The seller countered with a higher down payment and higher interest rate. . Linda held firm and only agreed to change the interest rate from 3 percent to 3.25 percent. Ultimately, they signed the final contract on those terms.

Because the contract included seller financing, they were able to close the transaction within 30 days. The seller was now able to move to a new city to work and used the income from the seller-financed note to qualify for a loan on a new house.

Note that the transaction would have been impossible if the seller was unable to satisfy his must-have: the price.

## SUMMARY OF TRANSACTION

### Step 1: Negotiation and Closing of Transaction

Buyer (Linda) → Offers the seller $125,000 with a $5,000 down payment, a 3 percent interest rate on the seller financing and a ten-year balloon

Seller → Counters for a higher down payment, a higher interest rate, and a shorter payoff time

Buyer (Linda) → Agrees to an increase in the interest rate from 3 percent to 3.25 percent

Buyer and Seller → Reach mutually acceptable contract

Buyer and Seller → Close the transaction within thirty days

**Step 2: Ownership of House**

Buyer (Linda) → Rents the house and receives a monthly cash flow

Buyer (Linda) → Continues to own the house as it gradually increases in value over the long term

## BENEFITS

**Benefit to Buyer:**

The buyer purchased the house for a small down payment and on acceptable terms.

The buyer received cash flow from renting the house.

The buyer built equity and value in the house over the long term.

The buyer moved one step closer to accomplishing the goal of owning fifty houses in five years.

**Benefit to Seller:**

The seller received his asking price and did not feel like someone had "taken advantage of him."

The seller was able to move to another city to accept a new job.

He seller also received monthly payments on the seller financing the he provided.

## Commercial or Investment Example

Two investors owned a vacant older commercial building in a highly desirable area of Fort Worth, Texas. The two investors had owned the property for several years and were disappointed that the property had not sold or been developed earlier. I knew one of the two investors very well and he asked me to look at the property and see what I could suggest to help them make money on the building.

The building itself required substantial remodeling in order to be rentable for any purpose. It had been a former gymnasium and had only a few alternative usages. Because the building had been a gymnasium with a large open basketball court, it had few limitations on the placement of walls or plumbing. The building also was extremely well constructed with a stronger-than-normal structural steel frame.

The rental market was slow due to a prolonged recession. The financing market was also extremely difficult due to both the effects of the recession on property values and the restrictions on bank financing imposed by the federal bank regulatory agencies.

An investment group that I managed decided to buy the building, remodel it, and sell the property as individual condominiums. One of the previous sellers had an outstanding plan to do that, but they had been unable to obtain financing. Our group decided to make an offer using seller financing. We initially made an all-cash discounted offer of $525,000 for the building. The offer was subject to our obtaining the financing that the sellers could not. Even though the sellers had been unsuccessful in obtaining financing, we had relationships with a number of banks that we felt would be interested in the deal.

The owner countered at $600,000, but gave us time to obtain financing for the purchase and the remodeling. We thought that the increase in price was a fair tradeoff for the increase in time.

After several months, however, it became clear that we would be unable to obtain any financing due to the economic conditions and the restrictions on banks making new loans. Every bank we went to told us the same sad story of federal restrictions on lending, which made it impossible for them to make this kind of loan. Our investment group saw that we had to change our plan.

## SOLUTION

We met with the sellers and explained the situation. While the sellers wanted all cash, they were willing to provide seller financing at a higher price. Together, we designed a new plan. We agreed to pay $630,000 for the property by assuming an existing first mortgage of $300,000 at a local bank and give the seller a $330,000 note for the balance of the purchase price. The note would be at no interest and due in full at the time of our refinancing.

The new plan was now to buy and hold the building until the condominium market and the financing market changed. We expected to make a substantial profit once the market rebounded.

Our investment group closed on the purchase of the property under this new business plan.

## SUMMARY OF TRANSACTION

**Step 1: Close on Purchase of Building**

Investment Group → Assumes existing first mortgage of $300,000 with bank.

Investment Group → Gives the seller an unsecured $330,000 note for the balance of purchase price.

### Step 2: Investment Group Owns the Building

Investment Group → Holds the building until the condominium market and the financing market improve.

## BENEFITS

### Benefits to Seller:

The seller is relieved of loan payments, taxes, and other costs.

The seller has a future receivable for equity in the building.

### Benefits to Investment Group:

The investment group acquires property with a substantial financial upside.

The investment group acquires property with no cash down payment (except closing costs).

The investment group has a potential development project for the future.

## KEY POINTS

Get clear about the facts about the other parties involved, not just the real estate. These are two of the fundamental principles of creative real estate.

Always make written offers.

Start with a basic seller financing framework and then add variations to create the net benefits needed by the parties to the transaction.

Look for ways to adjust the terms to solve problems as they arise in the negotiation.

Look for the terms each party must have in order to close a deal. Once you have identified the terms you must have in the transaction, do not sacrifice what you really need just to make a deal.

# NEGOTIATE FINANCING TERMS TO INCREASE VALUE

## Strategy

When the seller's price and the market value do not match, you can negotiate on the financing terms so that both parties win. Said another way, you can structure the deal so that each party receives sufficient benefits to motivate them to act. Of course, to determine how any change of the terms will affect the other parties to a transaction requires getting to know the people. In fact, the principle of creating relationships is critical to understanding the seller's wants and needs to create a mutually acceptable deal.

For example, a change in the amount of the down payment or a change in the interest rate on any seller-financed transaction can provide additional benefits to both the buyer and the seller. These kinds of changes in the terms of the seller financing can offset an initial concern about the price. All the terms in the real estate contract and financing are malleable (shapeable) to produce additional benefits.

Let's look at how some of the terms to a seller-financed mortgage could be altered to change the benefits available to the respective parties. For example,

- The price could be increased or decreased.

- The interest rate could be increased or decreased during the term of the loan.

- The payments could be low, high, or change over time.

- The loan could be secured by the property being sold, by another property, or by nothing at all.

- The loan could provide for a release of part of the property secured by the mortgage once the loan declines to a certain level.

- The loan could provide for a balloon payment under certain circumstances. For example, the length of time until the balloon payment could be months or years, depending on the situation and the size of the payment.

Changes in these terms could also be made in various combinations.

For example, the price and amount of seller financing could be increased by reducing the interest rate on the loan. This would result in the seller having more long-term taxable gain at the time of sale, but less ordinary income from interest over the life of the loan. A seller may find this attractive if he or she expected an increase in ordinary income in the years ahead. The seller would then be reducing the overall tax he or she expected to pay for the entire transaction, including both the sale and the collection of interest payments on the seller-financed note.

This may not be a significant change for the buyer, but could be very attractive for the seller.

Alternatively, the buyer could make a larger down payment in return for a reduction of the purchase price. This would also naturally reduce the amount of any seller financing. The seller may be willing to accept a lower price if they are receiving a sizeable amount of cash at closing. The buyer is sacrificing the opportunity cost of using a larger amount of their cash in return for the better price on the property.

This is what I mean when I say the structure of the terms of the transaction and seller financing are malleable to produce the maximum benefits for *both* parties.

The following examples document how this works in actual transactions.

## Residential Example

A couple had owned a number of very nice rental homes in the Dallas–Fort Worth area. They prided themselves on owning attractive and well-maintained properties.

One property they owned had been the subject of a long, complex legal eviction case with a tenant. They finally took possession of the property from the tenant and found it in extremely poor condition. The condition of the house was so poor that it was extremely embarrassing.

The sellers wanted out because they did not want to deal with all the problems they feared would come out of the bad condition of the house in addition to the potential damage to their image in the community.

Like many other sellers in this kind of situation, they would rather transfer their problems to someone else even if it means reducing their price and selling at a loss. When buyers say they want to "add value" (in return for a profit), they are often taking on the real or perceived problems of those type of sellers.

The couple listed the vacant rental house with a traditional real estate broker at $169,000, approximately $56,000 less than the "as remodeled value" of $225,000. Although the sellers knew the remodeled value of the house was substantially higher, they believed that the house was going to take a substantial amount of time, work, and money to be saleable.

## SOLUTION

A remodeler I know was looking for a fix-up opportunity that would require a minimum cash investment. She was looking to use her knowledge, skills, and "sweat equity" to make the maximum profit while investing the minimum amount of cash.

The remodeler inspected the vacant house and quickly became very interested in the property. It was in her "target area," which is the geographical area in which she wanted to focus her investments.

She had chosen her target area after careful consideration of many important factors: condition of both owner-occupied and renter-occupied housing, overall property values, rental rates, demographic trends, and distance she had to travel from her home and office.

The house itself did have very poor "curb appeal" because of various exterior issues. The exterior trim was damaged in various places, the paint was cracked and peeling, and some of the gutters and downspouts were hanging haphazardly off the sides of the roof. The bushes were not trimmed, the trees had dead and broken limbs, and the lawn had bare spots and weeds. A structural support on the front porch was also damaged.

While as a whole these items were overwhelming to the seller, each of these items was solvable at minimal expense.

The interior of the house was in good condition. The house had been cleaned, the walls had been quickly repainted when the tenant had moved out, the carpet had been steam cleaned, and various broken items in the interior had been repaired.

The remodeler offered to purchase the house for $150,000, which was $19,000 below the listing price. The contract was as follows: $10,000 cash down, assumption of the $64,000 loan, and a nine-month note of $76,000 for the balance. The remodeler offered to secure the $76,000 note with a second mortgage on the house with the balance all due and payable in nine months with no interest.

The sellers countered the original offer, but the buyer refused to budge. While the sellers wanted a higher price, they were motivated to sell quickly. Ultimately, the sellers accepted the original offer. (Notice that what a person wants and what a motivated person will actually do are two very different things.)

The remodeler closed the purchase of the house and quickly went to work. She spent approximately $25,000 to remodel and pay for owner-ship costs (such as utilities, maintenance, and taxes) during that period. When the work was completed, the house sold within a few weeks for $225,000, which gave her a net profit of approximately $35,000. The transaction was simple and highly effective.

The $76,000 second mortgage was especially important to the remodeler in the transaction. If she had been required to obtain the secondary financing market, both the availability and cost of such financing would have made the transaction untenable.

With the $76,000 second mortgage, the transaction as designed was acceptable to the remodeler.

Since the remodeler had to pay the monthly ownership costs while re-modeling the house, she made the remodeling a priority in her life so that she could complete it as quickly as possible and cut down on the carrying costs during remodeling. If remodeling is more expensive than you have budgeted, or you run out of cash, this can delay completion of the remodeling and extend the time when you are carrying the house without any rental income or cash from the sale.

Be realistic in calculating both the time and the costs to remodel a property, as well as covering the costs of ownership during the remodeling and sales period. If you are new at remodeling, it could take you considerably more time that an experienced remodeler. Consider that in your estimates.

## SUMMARY OF TRANSACTION

### Step 1: Close the Purchase of the House

Buyer → Pays $10,000 cash down payment to the seller

Buyer → Assumes $64,000 loan obligation of the seller

Buyer → Gives $76,000 note to the seller with no interest due for nine months

Seller → Gives deed to the house to the buyer

### Benefits

### Benefits to Seller:

The seller received $10,000 cash at closing (less closing costs).

The seller received a release of liability on the $64,000 first mortgage.

The seller was relieved of the monthly payments and ownership costs on the house.

The seller was also relieved of the burden of having to remodel the property.

The seller received the balance of the purchase price at the time of the sale of the house (nine months maximum).

## BENEFITS TO BUYER REMODELER

The buyer bought the house with a small down payment (which she recouped in the refinancing).

The buyer made a profit on remodeling and reselling the property.

The buyer did not have to pay interest or points on the loan from the seller, saving thousands of dollars.

## Commercial or Investment Example

An architect and his wife owned a newer, luxury duplex (two adjoining units) they had built. Both sides of the duplex were rented to tenants. They were offering the duplex for sale at $390,000. The duplex had cost them $370,000 to build, but the market value was only about $330,000. The property's market value was less than its actual cost. This was because the overall market had dropped and because the architect had over designed the duplex for the neighborhood in which it was located.

Because the list price was so far above the current market prices, they had absolutely no offers from qualified buyers.

## Solution

I first found the property on the expired listing list. The listing had been active for 297 days. The length of the days on market first sparked my interest. I have found that the longer a property goes unsold, the more likely the seller is motivated to agree to a creative sale.

I called the sellers and learned that they still wanted to sell the property. I arranged a meeting to view the duplex and, more importantly, talk to the sellers face to face. Remember the principle: "It's about the people, not just the property."

I met the seller/architect at the property and toured the property with the consent of the tenants.

I found the duplex was excellently built. The framing of the house was 12 inches "on center." That means that the studs on the exterior and interior walls were all spaced at 12-inch intervals. This is a much higher standard than typical construction. The attic insulation was rated at R49, a much higher rating than the weather conditions of the region required. All the doors, appliances, hardware, and carpet matched this high level of construction. The architect/seller had truly built a monument to his architectural vision. He was very proud of his creation! He wanted me to understand what he had put into the design and construction of the duplex. He also wanted to prove to me why the price of $390,000 was justified.

By talking with him, I also learned the other reason the property had been listed at $390,000. When the architect had originally proposed to his wife that they build the duplex, he had promised her that they would not lose money building the duplex. Therefore, he priced it $20,000 above the $370,000 cost to build. This was despite the lack of interest shown by buyers when the property had been listed with an agent.

After determining the true motivations of the architect/husband, I (the first buyer) offered to purchase the property for $390,000. The terms of the purchase agreement I proposed were $15,000 as a down-payment, the assumption of an existing $270,000 conventional first mortgage, and a $105,000 seller-financed second mortgage at increasing interest rate (1 percent interest the first year, 2 percent the third, 3 percent, etc. until rate reached 8 percent in year eight, then amortized over twenty years thereafter).

You will notice that I structured the purchase agreement to give the sellers the price they wanted while giving myself good long-term benefits from the financing I proposed. The seller countered the terms of the transaction several times, at first requiring a higher down payment and then later increasing the interest rate on the seller-financed second mortgage. I had a number of follow up meetings with both of the sellers, each time showing them I could not alter the terms without dropping the purchase price. Finally, the architect and his wife accepted the inevitable and signed the purchase contract.

The existing first mortgage was with a local bank at 7 percent interest and amortized over a remaining twenty-three years. That existing first mortgage was a good long-term loan that I wanted to assume and keep in place.

How did I get the bank to allow me to assume the existing first mortgage? I went in and asked them! I sat down with the bank's loan officer who was accountable for the loan and convinced him I would be a good customer for the bank. I brought all my financial information and my cash flow projections on owning the house. I also began building a personal relationship with the loan officer. Ultimately, the bank approved my assumption of the loan.

## THE REST OF THE STORY

As the "first buyer," I owned the duplex for two years and received a positive cash flow from the investment. This was substantially due to the low interest rate and low monthly payment on the second mortgage. Because of the superior construction quality, there was also little maintenance required. The resulting positive cash flow was a substantial benefit to me.

After those two years, I sold the duplex to an investor for $375,000 with a $15,000 down payment and a 9 percent interest, twenty-year, $360,000 all-inclusive wrap-around mortgage with no prepayment allowed. In the third year after my original purchase and the first year of my resale, I was receiving 9 percent interest on the all-inclusive wrap-around mortgage and paying 7% interest on the underlying first mortgage and 3 percent interest on the second mortgage. Although the interest rate on the second mortgage increased each year, from the third through the ninth year, I would receive the benefit of that interest rate differential.

Note: An all-inclusive note is a loan in which the underlying first loan is not paid off, but remains in place with the new buyer (investor) making a monthly payment to the current seller (me) and the current seller (again me) remaining responsible for the payment on the first and second mortgages. Because many institutional loans have a prohibition about selling property without paying off the first loan, a buyer or seller should consult with an attorney before entering into this kind of contract.

You will notice later that, despite the sale price being lower than my original purchase price, I still made a profit because of the benefits I structured for myself on the terms of the sale. The terms of the sale provided positive cash flow to me as the first owner, again because of the interest rate difference of the all-inclusive note and the underlying financing. I was collecting more interest than I was paying.

In this transaction, the investor personally guaranteed the terms and conditions of the all-inclusive note. The investor was a successful doctor who was buying investment real estate as his retirement program. Thus, the personal guarantee by him of the all-inclusive note provided real benefit to me. A personal guarantee by a person with both a high net worth and with substantial personal income provided a greater reliability that the payments and entire principal would be repaid in full.

The bank that held the underlying first mortgage also approved the transaction. After all, the bank had not only me "on the hook" for the loan, but also the investor/doctor. The original sellers had no say on the transaction as I had carefully crafted the second mortgage such that there was no "due on sale" when I transferred title to the property. Again, everything in a real estate transaction is negotiable.

Three years later, the duplex had increased in value and lower interest rates were available from refinancing. The investor wanted to pay off the underlying financing to take advantage of both receiving cash from the refinancing proceeds and the benefit of lower interest rates. Because the all-inclusive note contained a prohibition against pre-payment, the investor could not pay off the all-inclusive note without the note holder's (my) permission. As the holder of the all-inclusive wrap-around mortgage, I declined to accept a payoff. That would have substantially reduced my cash flow and profit! The bottom line is that I did not agree to a payoff of the loan. That provision for no prepayment of the loan was my negotiating a transaction that gave me net benefits in that original transaction. Without that provision, I would not have sold the property to the investor in the first place.

After extensive negotiations, the Investor paid a $25,000 cash premium to purchase the all-inclusive wrap-around mortgage and complete the refinancing. In other words, the investor paid $25,000 more than the balance of the loan for a release.

The investor did that because the new mortgage payment was still much lower than the old payment. The investor would still have a higher cash flow even after paying the cash premium than with the previous all-inclusive note with me. I held firm because this was how I had structured my profit in the original sale to the investor. Without that one provision, I would have actually lost money on the sale.

## SUMMARY OF TRANSACTION

### Step 1: Close Purchase on Easy Terms

First buyer (me) → Pays a $15,000 down payment to the seller (first owners)

First buyer (me) → Assumes $270,000 first mortgage

First buyer (me) → Gives $105,000 second mortgage to the seller (first owners)

First buyer (me) → Gives deed for duplex to the buyer

**Step 2: First Buyer Receives Cash Flow**

First buyer (me) → Receives cash flow on ownership of duplex for two years

**Step 3: First Buyer Sells to Investor/Second Buyer**

Investor → Pays $15,000 down-payment to the first buyer (me)

Investor → Gives $360,000 all-inclusive note to the first buyer (me)

First buyer (me) → Gives deed to the investor

**Step 4: First Buyer Receives Cash Flow**

First buyer (me) → Receives a positive cash flow on all-inclusive note for two years

**Step 5: Payoff of All-Inclusive Note**

Investor → Refinances property

First buyer (me) → Receives payoff of the all-inclusive note from the investor

First buyer (me) → Receives $25,000 cash premium on payoff of the all-inclusive note from the investor

First buyer (me) → Simultaneously pays off the underlying first and second mortgage

## BENEFITS

**Benefits to Seller (Architect and Wife):**

The architect got to justify himself with his wife about them not losing any money on the construction. (Never underestimate this powerful motivation!)

The architect and his wife eventually received back all the money they had invested in building the duplex.

**Benefits to First Buyers (Me):**

Buyer obtained an investment in a newer property with a small positive cash flow and strong future appreciation.

Buyer received positive cash flow for a total of four years (two years of owning the property and two years of owning the all-inclusive loan).

Buyer exchanged the cash flow to be received over future years (profit later) for the $25,000 premium (profit now).

Buyer made a profit—even though the property sold for less than what was originally paid. (This is a clear demonstration of the difference between "price" and "benefits.")

**Benefits to the Investor:**

The investor added property to his investment portfolio with only a small down payment.

The investor received some cash flow during his ownership plus substantial depreciation benefits.

The investor received cash refinancing proceeds.

The investor ultimately increased the cash flow on the duplex by reducing the interest rate and payment on the mortgage.

## KEY POINTS

There are many ways to adjust the terms of seller financing to improve the benefits in a transaction. You can "structure" the deal so that all parties receive sufficient benefits to motivate them to act.

You never know what people will really do until you make an offer. You also never know what *you* will really do until you are presented with an offer or a counteroffer. A seller-financed note may actually provide more benefits than any other type of transaction. That note can be negotiated to be secured by the property, secured by other property, or even unsecured. The interest rate could be low or it could be high. The due date on the note could be long term or short term. The payments could be low or high. There are many possible variations, which can increase the net benefits in the transaction to make it acceptable to all parties.

Create a relationship with the other party as you explore and as you negotiate. In many cases, they can be then become partners in other deals if they trust you to honor their benefits as well as your own.

If you carefully examine another party's motivation, you can offer creative financing terms that can fit their motivation and your transaction requirements.

# OWNER-FINANCE AND SELL (OR FINANCE) THE NOTE

## STRATEGY

As a seller, what if you could find a way to get all cash from the sale of a property and still be able to help buyers who have little cash of their own be able to buy?

As a buyer, what if you could buy a property you want without already having the cash up front that the seller wants at closing.

Sounds like a fantasy, doesn't it?

Where the buyer has limited cash for a down payment and the seller needs cash from the closing, using a seller-financed mortgage can still work in this difficult scenario. The seller can accept a purchase contract for the property that still includes seller financing by inserting a special condition in the contract. The special condition stipulates that the sale of the property is subject to being able to sell the seller-financed mortgage and close that sale immediately following the sale of the property. By doing so, the seller is able to still receive the cash he or she needs after the closing.

This requires finding a third party who will buy that mortgage right at the closing so that the seller gets the cash that is needed from the sale. This new third party now owns the mortgage and collects the payments.

Frequently a buyer of mortgages will require a discount from the seller on the purchase of the note, but not always. The amount of the discount depends on many factors, such as the total amount of the note, the loan to value, the interest rate, the state of the overall economy, and the specific real estate market. There is no real way for me to address the amount of the discount that might be required. I recommend that you analyze the transaction as a whole as part of your real estate decision-making. Furthermore, I will caution that just because the individual factors look good, this does not mean the transaction as a whole will work for you.

Again, this is where a knowledgeable professional can help. You will want to carefully select a closing agent who is capable and knowledgeable about escrow closings and train this individual in exactly how you would like to work with him or her to close any transaction that takes more than a single closing.

## Residential Example

I was marketing a house I owned. It was in an older neighborhood that included some older industrial buildings. Houses in the neighborhood were not in high demand because of the semi-industrial nature of the area.

I had bought the house several months before at a price of $70,000 and had invested approximately $10,000 into remodeling it. Overall, I had $80,000 in total cost in the property. The appraised value of the remodeled house was $120,000.

I had originally been prepared to substantially discount the sales price of the house to $100,000 under an all cash/quick close deal. Then a buyer came along who would pay full price, all cash, but the offer was subject to their obtaining financing. Together, we estimated the time required to complete the financing was approximately ninety days.

I accepted the contract to sell the house for a price of $120,000 with the financing contingency. After all, it was a full-price offer.

The buyers were a young couple with good jobs and decent credit. They were putting $10,000 down and had applied for a $110,000 new first mortgage at 5 percent interest. They really wanted to buy the house. Although the neighborhood was "iffy," it was so close to the husband's work that he could walk to work every day. This saved the cost of buying a second vehicle. The house was also priced at a point where they could easily afford the payments.

At the last minute, the potential lender for the couple buying the house decided against making the loan because of the industrial nature of the neighborhood. The neighborhood was also not a favorite of other lending institutions. I had a problem and little time to solve it. Furthermore, I realized that it could take months to find another all-cash, full-price buyer for this house in a transitional neighborhood.

## SOLUTION

I talked with the potential buyers. They were very upset, as the house really worked for them. After several hours of negotiation, they reached a new agreement.

I agreed that I would sell them the house for the same purchase price of $120,000 with seller financing of $110,000. The terms of the seller financing would be a higher interest rate of 7 percent interest amortized over twenty years. I also gave them the right to pay off the loan at any time. Finally, I agreed to give the buyers a $5,000 discount if they paid off the loan within three years.

While the 7 percent interest rate was higher than the 5 percent market interest rate with the potential lender, the buyers saw this as an acceptable cost to pay for a short period in order to buy the house they really wanted. The buyers also loved the opportunity to get the $5,000 discount by paying the loan off early, as they believed they could refinance the house long before that time. By refinancing, they would get a lower interest rate, a lower payment, and the $5,000 discount.

I did make the contract subject to being able to sell the seller-financed mortgage immediately following the closing with the buyers. I did this by simply writing a paragraph into the contract that stated, "This contract is subject to seller negotiating a firm contract to sell the first mortgage from the buyer to a third party on or before three days prior to closing. In the event that seller is unable to reached a firm agreement to sell the first mortgage to a third party, then seller may cancel this contract by giving written notice."

I went to a local insurance claims attorney who would sometimes buy mortgages at discount from people. I had conducted some business with him in the past and knew him to be a reliable source of money. The attorney offered to buy the $110,000 carry-back note at a discounted price of $94,000. While I would be discounting the note by $16,000, it was still acceptable since I was getting full price on the property itself.

That gave the note buyer the interest on the loan plus a profit of an additional $11,000 if the buyers paid the loan off early ($16,000 discount on his purchase of the note less the $5,000 discount to the buyers for paying off the loan early). If the buyers did not pay off the loan early, the note buyer would receive the full-face amount of the note, including that $5,000, but over a longer period of time.

I had been prepared to take a discount on the price of the house for an all cash/quick close sale. Instead of taking a discount on the price of the house, I took a discount on the sale of the seller-financed note. The result was virtually the same as selling the house at a discount for a quick close.

If you remember from the beginning of this example, I had $80,000 invested in the property. I sold the property for $120,000. On the sale of the Seller-Financed note, I took a $16,000 discount. Ignoring transaction costs, my net profit was $24,000, as follows:

$120,000 Sales Price

-$ 80,000 Total Cost

-$ 16,000 Note Discount

$ 24,000 Net Profit

## Summary of Transaction

**Step 1: House Closing**

Buyer → Pays the seller (me) $10,000 cash down payment

Buyer → Gives the seller (me) $110,000 seller-financed note for the balance of the $120,000 purchase price

Buyer → Gives the seller (me) a first mortgage on the house to secure the $110,000 seller-financed note

Seller → Deeds house to the buyer

**Step 2: Sale of Note (Immediately Following Closing):**

Seller (me) → Assigns $110,000 note to the note buyer

Seller (Me) → Receives $94,000 from the note buyer

## Benefits

**Benefit to Buyer:**

The buyers got the home they really wanted. It was something they could afford in a neighborhood close to their work. They were very happy for that.

The slightly higher interest rate cost them a little more per month in payments for a little over two years. They refinanced the house with a local lender and reduced both their interest rate and their payments.

**Benefit to Note Buyer (Insurance Claims Attorney):**

The note buyer ultimately received more than a 13.9 percent return as he received his principal back early.

The note buyer also had a first mortgage on the property, which is a very secure lending position.

**Benefit to Seller (Me):**

I paid off the bank on time and as agreed. That increased my reputation with the bank for future deals.

I made the note buyer very happy with this very solid deal. That increased my reputation with him for future loans.

I still made a profit of $24,000 on the transaction.

I sold the house sooner and was able to have cash for another deal.

## Commercial or Investment Example

A friend of mine owned a parcel of commercial land in Michigan. He had it on the market at a price of $142,500. The town in which the land was located was small and located near a national park. A national private prison company was building a new prison in the town and expected to open the facility the following year.

I recognized that there were no quality hotels or motels in the vicinity and that this property would make an excellent hotel site once the construction of the local prison was completed.

Overall, there are a number of potential overnight visitors whenever a prison is opened People come to visit their family members and friends when they are in prison. Vendors come to make sales and deliveries. Administrators and inspectors come to perform various tasks.

I asked my friend who owned the land to join me in the development of the hotel. My friend was willing, but he wanted some financial commitment on my part.

## Solution

My friend offered to sell me one-half interest in the property entirely for a note of $72,500 secured only by the one-half interest I was buying. In that way, I would be making monthly payments and paying my 50 percent share of the taxes. I agreed, if I received the exclusive development rights on the property for the hotel through my 50 percent ownership.

Before we did the transaction, my friend had a loan that he owed to a local bank of approximately $50,000 secured by the entire parcel of land. Simultaneous with the closing of our deal, he had his bank release the mortgage on the half interest in the property I was buying and, instead, secure the loan with the note that I had given him and the other half interest in the land that he already owned.

Said another way, he financed the carry-back note I gave him with his local bank and paid off his existing financing. The payments that I made to my friend then went to his bank to pay on his loan.

Where a seller requires cash from a transaction and a buyer wants a potential development deal for minimal investment, the strategy of one-half seller financing and sell (or finance) the note can save the day!

The buyer gets terms on the note given for the 50 percent ownership and the seller gets cash by selling or obtaining financing using the note. In addition, the terms of the note can always be adjusted to meet the purchase or financing requirements of a third party lender. If the lender needs a higher interest rate to make the deal, the note can be adjusted in the transaction.

The buyer and the lender may even negotiate other terms of the transaction to make it acceptable to both of them. As long as the seller gets the cash required from the transaction (or avoids paying out cash in the transaction, as in this case), he or she may be willing to be more flexible on the terms.

In our case, we closed the transaction and began doing the work to develop the hotel.

## SUMMARY OF TRANSACTION

### Step 1: Land Closing

Buyer → Gives $72,500 note to the seller

Seller → Deeds one-half interest in the land to the buyer and agrees to give me exclusive development rights

**Step 2: Assignment of Note**

Seller → Assigns $72,500 note as collateral to the bank for his note

My friend's bank → Releases the one-half interest in the land for the new buyer

## Benefits

**Benefits to Seller (My Friend):**

My friend created "activity" on his overall development.

My friend created income from my note to cover his debt service. One-half of the taxes were also covered.

My friend ended up with the potential for an interest in the future hotel development.

**Benefits to Buyer (Me):**

I got a local partner for a future hotel development. This was highly important. A local partner provides the "boots on the ground" to handle issues as they arise. It is very beneficial to have someone who is in the local area to attend zoning meetings, meet with contractors, and even be alert to local rumors that would be detrimental or beneficial to a development.

I got control of the land with no initial cash investment.

## Key Points

Mortgage note buyers can help you make a transaction where the buyer has little cash and the seller requires all cash.

The ability to sell or finance the note gives more flexibility to all parties in the transaction. It adds one more tool in using seller financing to complete a successful transaction.

The ability to sell or finance the seller-financed note depends directly on the terms of that note. Is it secured by a first or second mortgage? What is the interest rate? What are the amounts and schedule of payments? Is there a date when the note is due and payable in full or is it a fully amortized note? All of these terms affect the sale value and ability to finance the note. If the terms of the note are changed, the ability to sell or finance the note changes as well.

Carefully select a closing agent who is capable and knowledgeable about escrow closings and train this individual in exactly how you would like to work with him or her to close any transaction that takes more than a single closing.

# SUBORDINATE THE CARRY-BACK FINANCING

## Strategy

Having a small down payment can sometimes be more important for the buyer of a property than having a low price. When you can minimize your cash outlays, you dramatically increase your return on investment. Part of having a high return on your investment is by having as little of your own money invested in the deal as possible. You do that by using other people's money to make money. Doing this allows you to spread your down-payment money and remodeling money over a larger number of deals.

Sometimes, there are a limited number of potential buyers for certain types of property. For example, a residential property in obvious disrepair is not desirable to most buyers. Older shopping centers, even with upgrade potential, are also frequently not in demand from investors. Older, vacant industrials buildings are not as attractive to a buyer as newer properties with existing tenants.

A new buyer, however, may be able to turn around a property where the owner cannot. The term "turn around" refers to improving a property through both investment and management. This implies the residential and commercial properties are designed for rental, but not operating consistent with their real potential. One way for the seller to make that kind of underperforming asset more attractive to a potential buyer is to provide a way for the buyer to have a low initial capital outlay. In that way, the buyer can use his or her money to invest in improvements to the property, instead of just the original purchase.

One way to reduce the down payment is by the seller *subordinating* the seller-financed note to a new first mortgage. That would mean that a financial institution or private investor could make a new mortgage and have *priority* over the seller-financed mortgage.

If the buyer guarantees that the money promised for improvements is actually spent on the improvements, the subordinated seller financing can actually be very safe for the seller. After all, the property should be worth substantially more with an upgrade to the property and new management. In the event that the seller ever did have to foreclose on the seller-financed mortgage, he or she should be getting back an even better asset. Of course, all of that is dependent upon the quality of the upgrades and management of the property as well.

Below are both a residential example and commercial/investment of the idea of subordinating the carry-back financing.

## RESIDENTIAL EXAMPLE

Imagine that you have located a residential property in terrible condition. The roof has leaks in it; the grass and weeds are waist high and the exterior trim needs repairs and painting. The foundation requires reconstruction. The taxes may even be in arrears.

In this example, the asking price is $115,000 all cash. The remodeled market value is $175,000, but it will take $30,000 and three months to clean and remodel the property and get it ready for sale. The owners own the house free and clear of all mortgages and are desperate to sell the property. They do not want to invest the time and money to fix the property up. The owners may even have bad memories of living there for a variety of reasons. The problem is do you want to invest your cash to both buy the property and remodel it for this amount of profit? This all comes back to the return on investment.

What could you do to improve the terms of the purchase to increase the return on investment?

## SOLUTION

As the buyer, you first have to educate the sellers as to why their price and terms on that particular property are not reasonable in the current market. If they are truly motivated to sell, they may listen to a well-reasoned argument for a lower price and better terms.

Once the seller is educated, you could offer to buy the property for $95,000 with a down payment of $30,000, and a carry-back note of $65,000. The next key step is to have the carry-back note be "subordinated to" (or behind) your bank's new loan to buy and remodel the property. That means that your bank's loan will be superior to the seller-financed second mortgage. This gives your bank the protection they may well require to make the loan in the first place.

Once you remodel and sell the property, both the bank's first mortgage and the seller's second mortgage will be paid off.

## SUMMARY OF TRANSACTION

### Step 1: Buyer Acquires House

Buyer → Negotiates a contract with the seller to buy the house for $95,000 with $30,000 cash down and a $65,000 carry-back subordinated second mortgage

Buyer → Obtains a first mortgage for $60,000 to cover the $30,000 down payment and the $30,000 remodeling cost

## Step 2: Buyer Remodels and Resells House

Buyer → Remodels the house

Buyer → Sells the house for $175,000 to the new buyer

Buyer → Pays off the first mortgage of $60,000 to the bank and the second mortgage of $65,000 to the seller

Buyer → Receives a gross profit of $50,000

## BENEFITS

### Benefits to Buyer:

The buyer can purchase the property for a very small or no actual down payment. (Ignoring closing costs on the original purchase the actual down payment from the buyer is actually "zero," even though the seller receives a down payment out of buyer's loan proceeds from the bank.)

The buyer's return on investment upon sale can be extremely high with little or no cash out of pocket.

The buyer has had most of the initial capital costs financed by the seller.

### Benefits to Seller:

The seller gets someone else to solve the problem for them.

The seller gets $30,000 cash at the time of the original closing.

The seller ultimately gets paid cash on sale.

## COMMERCIAL OR INVESTMENT EXAMPLE

An elderly seller had a small free and clear shopping center for sale with an owner value of $250,000. The shopping center had a substantial number of vacancies and some deferred maintenance.

Because of the substantial number of vacancies, the actual net operating income of the shopping center was only $15,000 per year. The potential net operating income was $40,000 per year with minor improvements and some sweat equity to lease the vacant spaces. (Note: In many cases, this sweat equity is the best way for new investors to get into real estate. Not only do new investors save money this way, but they can also gain valuable experience and new skills.)

The resulting increased occupancy and increased rental rates would be a potential market value for the repositioned shopping center of $400,000. This estimate is based upon a net operating income after expenses of $40,000 and a market yield (or capitalization rate) of 10 percent. The value calculation is as follows: $40,000 Net Operating Income divided by 10 percent (or $40,000 / 10%) = $400,000.

The seller was insistent on getting as close to $250,000 for the property as possible. He looked at the vacancy and reduced cash flow as only temporary, and did not believe these situations warranted a price reduction.

An interested developer had substantial assets and good credit but little cash for a down payment. The developer believed the shopping center could be turned around with a minor facelift and some sweat equity.

## Solution

The developer offered a purchase price of $225,000 for the shopping center as follows:

A) $125,000 cash down and a $100,000 carry-back second mortgage at 6 percent interest and

B) The $100,000 carry-back second mortgage was payable interest only for twenty years, at which time the balance of the note would be all due and payable. This gave the seller an income of $500 per month ($100,000 multiplied by 6 percent = $6,000 per year, which then divided by 12 months=$500 per month).

C) This carry-back financing provided by the seller would be a second mortgage *subordinated* to a new first mortgage of $175,000.

A local bank—that frequently provided funding for the developer—made a new first mortgage of $175,000 including $50,000 for improvements. The bank held the $50,000 for improvements in an escrow account at the bank until needed. Holding the $50,000 for improvements in an escrow protected the seller of the shopping center, as well as the bank, in making sure that the funds were actually spent for the intended improvements.

## Summary of Transaction

### Step 1: Developer Acquires the Shopping Center

Developer → Negotiates a contract with the seller to buy the shopping center for $225,000 with $125,000 cash down and a $100,000 carry-back second mortgage at 6 percent interest

Developer → Obtains a first mortgage for $175,000 to cover the $125,000 down payment and the $50,000 remodeling cost

Developer → Closes the transaction and places $50,000 into the escrow account for improvements to the shopping center

## Step 2: Developer Remodels and Rents the Shopping Center

Developer → Remodels the shopping center using the $50,000 improvement escrow

Developer → Rents the remaining vacancy of the shopping center at a higher rental rate

Developer → Creates cash flow and increased value through improvements, marketing, and real property management (i.e., sweat equity). (Note: Once the property is remodeled and repositioned, the developer can either hold the property as an investment or sell it to raise capital for future developments.)

## BENEFITS

**Benefit to Seller:**

The seller received $125,000 cash at closing.

The seller also received a $100,000 note payable at 6 percent interest. The note payments provided $500 per month cash flow to the seller.

The seller's security for the $100,000 carry-back financing was essentially the same as being the owner. The worst case was that the seller could foreclose on the second mortgage, get the property back with remodeling, and complete the remarketing of the property. The seller would then have both a good long-term loan in place and cash in the bank.

**Benefit to Buyer/Developer:**

The buyer/developer obtained a development opportunity for no equity investment.

The buyer/developer made a substantial profit from using sweat equity.

**Benefits to the Lender:**

The lender received a conservative loan position with a seasoned developer.

The lender kept a good customer working and making money.

The lender received the benefits of providing checking and savings accounts for the shopping center.

## KEY POINTS

In the "subordinate the carry-back financing" strategy, the buyer is able to reduce the capital outlays for a purchase, including both the costs at closing and the costs after the closing (for example, remodeling costs and carrying costs). This approach allows investors who prefer to provide sweat equity versus cash equity to acquire opportunities not otherwise available.

The sellers get their problems solved and ultimately get paid in cash. At the same time, the lenders have a conservative loan position.

Another method to accomplish a similar result is for the buyer to use *another* asset to secure the seller-financed portion of the purchase price.

## SUBORDINATE THE CARRY-BACK FINANCING

The developer in the commercial or investment situation could have provided separate collateral for the carry-back financing. For example, another well-performing asset of the developer could have secured the carry-back second mortgage. This could have been useful in the event the seller or lender found the other asset more acceptable.

By subordinating the carry-back financing, the seller allows the buyer to successfully buy and improve the property, which benefits all parties involved.

# SELL PROPERTY BY FINANCING FROM PARENTS, FAMILY, EMPLOYERS, OR FRIENDS

## STRATEGY

There are always people, businesses, and organizations indirectly affected by any transaction. I say indirectly because the impact may be minimal but still important. The trick is to spot the indirect players in the transaction. Those indirect players may well be the critical resource in the event you run into a problem making a transaction with a buyer or seller.

In residential situations, parents of both the buyers and sellers are an often-overlooked resource. While gifts from parents to children to buy a home are common, those mostly occur because the parents have cash in a savings account from which they could make the gift. If the parents do not have the money, that idea normally goes no further. How might you enable a buyer to purchase a property even if the parents do not have the cash?

Consider first that the parents are not the only source of gifts or financing assistance. Buyers may have other family and friends that could make a gift or a loan on other assets. Buyers have employers who may be able to provide money by paying a bonus or a lump sum advance on wages. And there are usually friends that can also provide assistance.

Parents, family, employers, and friends are a resource even when they do not have the immediate cash to give or loan to buyers. Their commitment to support the buyer and some other assets may all that is needed to provide the necessary funding. For example, they could have an asset that could be used as collateral for a loan, such as a single family home, a single-family lot, a car, even a recreational vehicle.

The same principle can apply in a commercial or investment situation. If you are or have a potential buyer for a commercial, industrial, or investment property who has an insufficient down payment, you can be proactive in closing the deal by searching for alternative sources of financing. Those alternate sources of funding do not need to have the cash immediately available either.

Assuming that the parties involved have explored all the available resources of the buyer, there are also the parents, family, employers, and friends of the seller as well. As long as any of those parties have a strong motivation to assist the buyer, a way can frequently be created to gain the funding needed.

One option, of course, is for the seller to make a legitimate loan directly to the buyer. Another option is for you as the seller to lend money to the buyer's parents, family, employers, or friends and then they can gift or lend the money to the buyer.

If *you* are the buyer for a residential, commercial, or investment property, you can also seek out an "angel" investor to help you buy the property, one who could possibly provide cash, collateral, or credit to assist your purchase.

The angel investor—whether parents, family, employers, or friends—may be also willing to take a lower return on investment out of their commitment for the buyer to get the property. In the end, providing that kind of support may benefits the angel investor either directly or indirectly. If there were no direct or indirect benefit, the angel investor would not make the loan in the first place.

Let us explore some examples of this strategy in action. Remember that the examples do not even begin to represent all of the different possibilities that are available to the buyer in any given situation.

## Residential Example

Consider the following scenario: Suppose you have a house for sale at $100,000, but you are willing to accept $90,000 in order to get it sold quickly.

A young couple with two children want to buy the house. Although they have excellent credit and sufficient income to make mortgage payments, they have no extra money for the down payment. Raising children is expensive!

As buyers, they are willing to pay full price, maybe even a premium, if they can find a way to buy the house. They need $10,000 cash for the down payment and closing costs.

In this case, they do not have proceeds coming from the sale of another house and they have no other property to finance. The husband does have parents who would be glad to do what they can to help, but they do not have an extra $10,000 available either. If their situation were different, they would give the cash to their son and his wife for the down payment and costs.

What could you do as the seller?

## Solution

Consider making a three-year $10,000 loan to the parents secured by their house. The parents can then can make a gift to their son and wife of $10,000 for the down payment and costs. The gift from the parents is an acceptable source of funds for almost every lender.

## SUMMARY OF TRANSACTION

**Step 1: Seller Makes Loan to Parents**

Seller → Lends $10,000 to the parents of the buyer

Seller → Receives mortgage secured by the parents' house

Buyer → Receives gift of $10,000 from parents

**Step 2: House Closing:**

Buyer → Pays $10,000 for down payment and closing costs

Buyer → Pays for balance of property with new loan

**Step 3: Payoff of $10,000 Loan**

Seller → Receives monthly payments on $10,000 loan from the parents. (Note: The interest rate and payments could be negotiated to fit the needs of both the parents and the seller.)

Seller → Receives $10,000 payoff in three years

## BENEFITS

**Benefits to Seller:**

The seller has a qualified buyer willing to sign a contract now for full price. The seller can complete the transaction, receiving $10,000 more than they were willing to take in the form of a three-year note from the parents.

Again, you have a sale at full price, making $10,000 more than you would on a discount sale.

## Benefits to Buyer (Young Couple):

The young couple can buy the house they need for the family now rather than waiting until they save up enough for the down payment and closing costs.

## Benefits to Parents of Young Couple:

The parents get to make a difference for their son and his wife, even if they currently lack the cash resources for the full down payment.

## Commercial or Investment Example

Early in my career, I owned a property that was in serious financial condition. I needed $100,000 to remodel the property and turn it profitable. My own bank would not make me a loan directly as I had little credit history and few quality assets. I tried a few other banks that turned me down as well. What to do? I needed help.

## Solution

I approached a business colleague. I had done a number of favors for him over the years and we had become friends. I told him my situation and he offered to help me out. He arranged a loan for me at a local bank and guaranteed the loan to the bank for me. He did not ask for anything in return. I would have given him a "financial incentive" to help me, but for him the "relationship incentive" was more important. Over the following years, we did a substantial amount of business together which greatly benefited both of us. Because of our relationship, he could call upon me when he was the one who needed special assistance.

## Summary of Transaction

**Step 1: Loan to Owner / Borrower (Me):**

Business colleague → Guarantees loan to the bank

Bank → Makes loan to me

## Benefits

**Benefits to Owner / Borrower (Me):**

I got the money needed to solve a problem.

**Benefits to Guarantor (Business Colleague):**

The guarantor did a good deed—a powerful motivator! He also built a strong business relationship with me, which has lasted even until now.

## Key Points

Never underestimate the willingness of family, friends, and business associates to provide the critical support to enable someone to acquire real estate. After all, those family, friends, and business associates have a stake in that person's success.

In many cases, the seller (or broker) does not have to be the one providing the financing, but rather simply suggesting the strategy to the buyer and letting them generate their own support.

It is important to remember that this is still a business transaction. Just because you are dealing with someone's family, friends, or business associates, do not assume that they will always keep their agreements. You must still document every piece of the transaction and protect your security interests in the appropriate ways. Perform the appropriate due diligence on the people, properties, and financial interests involved.

This would also be a good place to use a third-party loan facilitator to close the loan to the friend or family member.

# SELL PROPERTY BY FINANCING OTHER PROPERTY

## STRATEGY

The best sale you can make is always to someone who *really* is motivated to own the property, either for the property itself or for the benefits available in the transaction. That kind of strong motivation will often pave the way for a transaction even if the buyer does not have the cash or credit available at the time.

One way that the buyer can purchase the seller's property is for the seller to finance *other* property that the buyer owns. The buyer can use the loan proceeds to make the down payment on the real estate, create a reserve for monthly payments on the real estate mortgage, or pay off other debt in order to be able to better qualify for the real estate mortgage. The seller could either finance the buyer directly or find a way for someone else to provide financing to the buyer.

The loan might be secured or it might be unsecured. If secured, the security could be real estate or it could be personal property.

If it is real estate, it could be a primary home, a second home, a residential rental property, a commercial building, or single-family lots. The alternatives are endless.

That other property that could be used as security for a loan includes personal property, such as automobiles, trucks, RVs, boats, planes, appliances, office equipment, construction equipment, other heavy equipment, antiques, jewelry, art, books, furniture, mineral rights, hunting rights, access rights, easements, stocks, bonds, and insurance policies.

The security, whether real property or personal property, could include property in state or out of state (or even out of the country).

The possible variations and alternatives available are staggering. The parties to a transaction can discover what might be possible only by building a good relationship and talking about the alternatives available.

A residential example and a commercial/investment example of the strategy to sell property by financing other property are shown on the following pages.

## RESIDENTIAL EXAMPLE

A couple I was advising was under contract to purchase a "for sale by owner" house in Dallas. The seller was the estate of the previous owner. The contract price was $160,000, all cash. The appraised market value was $200,000 "as is." The couple stood the very real prospect of making a $40,000 profit with no cash investment!

As was their practice, my clients typically wanted to find a buyer prior to their own closing and "flip" the house to a new buyer. The house was rented to a tenant at the time and the lease did not end for nine months. They were unable to effectively negotiate with people looking to buy a home to move into, and that limited the buyers to investors who wanted a below-market price.

At my suggestion, they did ask for and got approval from the estate representative to talk to the tenant. They discovered that the tenant had good credit and would love to purchase the house, but had absolutely no cash for a down payment or closing costs. He was a single man and had moved from Arkansas for a job in Dallas.

## Solution

By asking questions of the tenant, my consulting clients also found that he owned a half-finished log cabin home in Arkansas that he was building himself with available cash and long weekends. The log cabin was his dream house to move into when he retired someday. The half-finished log cabin had a current market value of approximately $140,000. When completed, it would be worth approximately $200,000. The tenant, however, needed approximately $10,000 for kitchen and bathroom fixtures for the Arkansas house to make it minimally habitable.

The solution my clients created was to lend the Tenant $35,000 secured by his half-finished log cabin in Arkansas. That way, the tenant would have sufficient money for the down payment on the house owned by the estate. Since the Arkansas log cabin had no other loans against it, my clients' loan in was in first position.

They wrote two contracts:

The first contract was the sale of the Dallas house by my clients to the buyer (tenant) at $200,000 with a $20,000 down payment and $180,000 new first mortgage, *subject to* the tenant being able to sell or finance his half-finished house in Arkansas.

The second contract was the financing of the half-finished house in Arkansas by my clients to the tenant for $35,000 *subject to* my clients being able to sell their $200,000 house.

Each contract was conditional on the other contract.

Two contracts were used for several reasons. First, a clean contract is better for the lender. Second, neither contract could stand on its own without the other.

Under the contract, my clients would make a $40,000 profit on the purchase and resale of the Dallas house. They would simultaneously make a $35,000 loan on the Arkansas house.

My clients would also then receive monthly payments including interest and a payoff of the $35,000 mortgage on the mortgage on the Arkansas house in three years (when the tenant finished and financed or sold it.

This was a win-win-win for the estate, the tenant, and my clients.

## Summary of Transaction

**Step 1: First Seller (the Estate) Sells Dallas House to My Clients**

My clients → Give first sellers (the estate) $160,000 cash

First sellers (the estate) → Give my clients deed to Dallas house

**Step 2: Seller (My Clients) Lend Buyer Money to Purchase House**

Seller → Lends the buyer (tenant) $35,000 secured by the Arkansas property

Buyer (tenant) → Gives the my clients a first mortgage secured by the Arkansas property

Lender → Makes $180,000 loan to the buyer (tenant) on Dallas home

Buyer → Pays $180,000 from new loan plus $20,000 down payment (from seller's loan) to the seller for the new house

Seller → Deeds the Dallas house to the buyer

Buyer → Has $15,000 for left over for closing costs on new Dallas home and remodeling costs for the Arkansas house

Buyer → Gives lender first mortgage on the Dallas house

**Step 3: Buyer Payoff of $35,000 Loan on the Arkansas property**

Seller → Receives monthly payments on the $35,000 loan from buyer

Seller → Receives $35,000 payoff in three years

## BENEFITS

**Benefit to Buyer (Tenant):**

The buyer buys the house now where he wants to live.

The buyer actually lowers his monthly payment by owning instead of renting.

The buyer end ups with some extra cash to continue to build the house in Arkansas.

**Benefit to Seller (My Clients):**

My clients make a $40,000 gross profit by completing their simultaneous purchase and sale of the house. That gross profit would be in the form of the $35,000 note from the tenant and $5,000 cash remaining after the closing on the sale of the Dallas house.

My clients receive monthly income and a cash payoff at the end of three years.

My clients obtain the "know-how" to repeat the strategy over and over again.

## Commercial or Investment Example

A corporation I had formed to invest in residential rental units owned seven smaller residential rental properties that I had accumulated over a period of three years. All seven properties were each secured by first mortgages with various lenders as well as a long-term all-inclusive deed of trust of $86,000 with a local credit union. While the interest rate on the second mortgage was very low, it did restrict my ability to sell any individual property without paying off the entire loan.

One day, I received a personal visit from a vice president of the credit union, who told me the credit union was calling my loan and demanding it be paid off immediately.

The real estate market was terrible and the loan market was worse. How was I going to be able to pay off this loan and not lose all my residential units in foreclosure?

After my shock (really terror) disappeared, I ask the critical question: "Why?"

The vice president told me that the credit union was converting from being a state credit union to being a federal credit union, and that to complete the conversion, their entire loan portfolio needed to be 100 percent in compliance with their existing state charter. My loan was stopping the conversion because they had made errors in my original loan. The credit union made the loan to a corporation rather than an individual in violation of their charter and the loan amount was higher than their legal limits.

I quickly realized that, while I did have a problem, the credit union had a bigger problem. The personal visit by the credit union's vice-president was further proof of that. If I could help the credit union solve their problem, I could solve mine.

## SOLUTION

One of the properties I owned was an older, run-down, four-unit residential property located next to the railroad tracks in an industrial area. Because of the location and the condition, the rents were relatively low.

The four-unit property had a recent market value appraisal of $100,000. It also had a very low first loan of only $26,000 against it. It was, however, part of the blanket all-inclusive deed of trust with the credit union.

I found three individuals who owned investment properties. They typically held title to their properties as individuals but managed them together. I persuaded them to buy my four-unit property for full appraisal all cash. How did I do that in such a terrible market?

I told them I knew how they could get new second mortgages for them secured by three of their individual properties to buy my four-unit property and own it free and clear of any loans. In that way, they would then be free to borrow money from a bank secured by my four-unit property. Again, this was in a market where there was no available second mortgage financing. When they were clear that I could deliver this promise of new second mortgages, they signed a contract to purchase my four-unit property for full price.

Each of the three individual investors submitted individual loan applications to the credit union on their three different properties as collateral for new individual second mortgages of $30,000, each to be secured by their individual properties. The loans would qualify under the credit union's existing charter as they were below the legal limit and made to the investors as individuals.

After a review of their individual financial statements and credit reports, the credit union agreed to make the new loans to them.. That would allow them to buy my four-unit property, which it made it possible for me to pay off the credit union.

We closed on my sale of the four-unit property to the three investors. At this point, the three investors had a $10,000 net investment into the purchase ($100,000 purchase price minus the total of $90,000 they received in loans from the credit union).

With the $100,000 sale of the four-unit property plus $22,000 from my savings, I paid off the all-inclusive mortgage of $86,000 to the credit union and the existing first mortgage on the four-unit property of $26,000.

The three individual investors then took the "free and clear" four-unit property, along with a copy of the $100,000 appraisal, to their own bank, which made them a new loan of $60,000. After consideration of the $10,000 net cash they invested in the four-unit property, the three investors netted a total of $50,000 cash from the transaction.

By buying my property for full appraisal all cash, the three investors walked away with cash at the closing. They would not have had this cash otherwise because there was no conventional second mortgage financing available for their individual investment properties. The second mortgage money for their individual investment properties came from the credit union, mostly from my payoff of the $86,000 all-inclusive note. Without the incentive for the credit union to solve the issue my loans created for their charter, the credit union would probably not have

SELL PROPERTY BY FINANCING FROM PARENTS, FAMILY, EMPLOYERS, OR FRIENDS

made the second mortgage loans to them in the first place.

In essence, we used the already *existing* financing with the credit union to close the transaction. In addition, note that the credit union had no net money invested in the transaction. They received a payoff of loans slightly higher than the new loans that they made.

This entire transaction was completed in a market where there were few buyers and where there was (theoretically) no second mortgage financing available.

## SUMMARY OF TRANSACTION

### Step 1: Sell the Four-Unit Property by Providing Financing

Buyers (investors) → Pay seller $100,000 cash for the four-unit property

Seller → Deeds the four-unit property to the buyers

Seller → Pays off blanket mortgage of $86,000 to the credit union

Seller → Pays off the first mortgage to the bank with $14,000 from the transaction and an additional $12,000 from savings

Buyers (investors) →Receive $90,000 in loans from the credit union

Buyers (investors) → Give credit union second mortgages of $30,000 on each of their three individual properties

### Step 2: Buyers Borrow Money Secured by the Four-Unit Property

Buyers (investors) → Receive $60,000 loan from the bank

Buyers (investors) → Give the bank first mortgage secured by the four-unit property

Buyers (investors) → Net $50,000 cash after purchase of four-unit property ($90,000 from three second mortgages secured by their individual properties, plus $60,000 loan from bank secured by the four-unit property, minus the $100,000 purchase price for the four-unit property)

## BENEFITS

**Benefits to the Credit Union:**

The credit union replaced my loan, which was not compliant for their charter, with three new loans with three investors that were compliant.

The credit union was able to become a federally chartered credit union and increased the benefits it received by that move.

**Benefits to Buyers (Investors):**

The buyers got additional financing they could not have gotten in the market at the time on the properties they already owned.

The buyers walked away with cash in their pockets by financing the four-unit property that they acquired in the transaction.

**Benefits to Seller (Me):**

I extracted myself from what could have become a difficult situation with the credit union.

I sold the four-unit property for full price, all cash, in a market with few buyers and almost no financing.

I reduced my debt by the sale of the four-unit property.

Because I paid off the loan to the credit union, I actually increased my cash flow on my remaining property holdings.

I also developed my reputation with the credit union, my bank, and the buyers that I could make things happen. A good reputation is a valuable thing to have.

## KEY POINTS

In the "sell property by financing other property" strategy, you can use existing financing and existing lenders as assets in the transaction. A seller can realize a sale or a higher price on a property from a buyer who really wants to buy the property, but seemingly cannot.

The property being financed could be real estate, personal property, or even intangible property. Almost anything can be used as security for a loan.

Another key to this strategy is that you or others be *proactive* in marketing property by contacting active real estate investors and making offers to buyers, rather than waiting for buyers to make offers to you. A potential buyer may not even be interested in your property, but when approached by you, may be willing to buy, *all because of the benefits that they could derive from the financing.*

For example, when I needed cash for an investment, and approached a potential investor, they would often offer me the cash I needed *if* I would also purchase property they wanted to sell. Their property was a "must-take" to get the cash. I have often purchased these properties to get the cash, and then later was able to sell them for a profit and offset the cost I paid for the property.

# LOAN ON FUTURE SALES PROCEEDS

## STRATEGY

Imagine you are negotiating with a potential buyer to purchase a property from you as the seller. The buyer is pre-qualified for a loan on the purchase and seems genuinely motivated in conversations with you.

You are sure that you can reach a mutually agreeable price, but then the buyer says to you something like the following:

"You know, I would buy this property right now, but my down payment is coming from another property I have under contract to sell and is supposed to close in about 120 days. The contract is firm and they have made a substantial earnest money deposit, but they are not willing to close before then. Will you sign a contract to sell your property with a 120 day closing?"

You could say yes, but if you agree to the 120-day closing, any number of circumstances can happen that could derail your transaction actually being completed. The buyers for the other property could back out, the financing could fall through, some party to the transaction could lose a job, and or any one of a hundred different scenarios.

Obviously, you could say no. Then you must deal with finding another buyer for your property. If you are confident you can find that other buyer, you might logically pursue that.

However, what happens if you do not see another buyer on the horizon and you really want or need to get a transaction closed quickly?

When you find a buyer who also has a purchase contract from a buyer to sell their home or other property, you could use their future sale to close your sale to them *now*. How would you do that?

You could lend the money from your sale to the prospective buyer and secure the loan by their expected sale proceeds. That way, they can close right now on the purchase of the house you have for sale. The decision to make that loan must only be made with some real due diligence and risk analysis. After all, that buyer's sale of the other property is also subject to the same uncertainties concerning closing as any other real estate transaction. If the net benefits of the transactions are great enough, in some cases the risk may well be worth using the strategy.

## Residential Example

To illustrate how you can both increase your profits and increase the speed of your sale, consider the following example.

A seller has a 3 bedroom, 2 bathroom house for sale. The seller acquired the house sixty days earlier for $50,000 and has put $20,000 into remodeling the property. The house today has an "as remodeled" market value of $100,000. The seller wants to sell this house in order to continue investing in new "fix and flip" properties.

The only buyers actually willing to sign a contract today at the full price of $100,000 have a problem. The sale of their house, which is under a firm contract with good earnest money, will not close for another 120 days. They really need and want to move now, but they do not have the money for the down payment yet.

The buyers are fully qualified for a new $70,000 loan, and they are getting another $40,000 from the sale of their other house when it closes in 120 days. The buyers want the seller to also accept a 120-day closing so that they can get the contract of their other house closed. However, the seller wants to close a deal now, not later. This is the same scenario that we discussed earlier.

## Solution

Of course, one alternative is that the seller could list the house at a discounted price of $90,000 and sell it fairly quickly. The seller might even expect to close in thirty to sixty days. After closing costs of $9,000, the seller would still net $11,000 cash. Sounds good, yes?

What if, instead of selling at a discount price, the seller could receive full price and close soon? They would make $10,000 more with that strategy more quickly and easily.

Here is one way the seller could do that. The seller could lend the buyer money now on the house they are selling until their other sale closes. That way, the buyers can close now on the house that the seller has for sale. Furthermore, the seller could secure the loan they would be making to the buyers by the house their buyers are selling (and indirectly the money they will be receiving at the time of its sale).

By lending the money to the buyer, they can close the purchase on the house the seller has on the market and simultaneously give the seller a note back secured by the proceeds from the house on which they have a contract to sell. The seller now has a note to be paid off in approximately 120 days with cash sale proceeds, and a $10,000 higher profit.

## Summary of Transaction

**Step 1: Loan on Other House:**

Seller → Lends the buyer $40,000 on the future sales proceeds

Buyer → Gives the seller a second mortgage on the other house

**Step 2: Sale of House:**

Buyer → Pays $100,000 for the house

Seller → Deeds the house to the buyer

Lender → Makes a $70,000 loan to the buyer

Buyer → Gives the lender a first mortgage on the house

Buyer → Pays the closing expenses

**Step 3: Repayment of Loan:**

Buyer → Pays off the $40,000 loan to the seller (upon sale of the other house)

## BENEFITS

**Benefit to the Buyer:**

The buyers can use their contracted sale to buy a house now rather than later.

The buyers can move into the new house immediately.

**Benefit to Seller:**

The seller has a sure sale now with real cash coming in a relatively short time.

The seller makes $10,000 extra by being creative.

## COMMERCIAL OR INVESTMENT EXAMPLE

The same strategy applies where the property being offered is a commercial or investment property.

Imagine a seller has a small vacant commercial building for sale. The price is $300,000 based upon a year-old appraisal. The bank loan is $150,000. Although the seller is current with the bank, the bank is nervous because the building has been vacant for more than nine months and the insurance policy will not cover any major losses because of the property's vacancy history.

The seller has offered the building for sale for more than a year with no legitimate offers. While there have been a few deeply discounted offers, the seller has been unwilling to accept such low offers. However, the seller has now begun to consider discounting the property to get it sold.

Suddenly, the seller is approached by a retailer that owns a retail store in a similar building on a nearby street. At last, a legitimate buyer!

The retailer's existing location has poor parking and access, and is not on as busy a street as the building for sale. The seller's building would be a substantial upgrade for the retailer's business. The retailer knows that the new building would increase customer sales and profits, and he is anxious to buy it.

The retailer does have a cash contract to sell his building to the company that owns an adjacent property. That company plans to use the adjacent property for expansion of business. The sales price is $180,000. Since the retailer has no loan against his property, his net sales proceeds would be approximately $165,000 after paying a real estate commission and closing costs.

What is the hitch? Yes, there is frequently a hitch.

While the company buying the retailer's building has written a firm contract, the closing is not until after the Christmas season is over. That way, the company will be in a better cash position to purchase that property. However, this is July, and that is almost six months in the future.

While the retail business of the retailer is still good, he does not have the cash reserves to purchase the building without the cash from the sale of his own building. In addition, he needs to hoard his cash to stock up on inventory for the upcoming Christmas season.

On the surface, it might look like there is nothing to do but wait for that other sale. Nevertheless, using the strategy we have been reviewing, the retailer could write a contract and close the sale of the building almost immediately.

Here is how!

## SOLUTION

The seller could propose a standard purchase contract on his building to the retailer as the buyer for the full retail price (not discounted). The contract could include paragraphs that simply state conditions for closing, such as "this contract is subject to buyer borrowing $150,000 on an existing property located at . . ." and "this contract is further subject to buyer borrowing $150,000 secured by the property being transferred to buyer by seller, or obtaining a new loan of equal or greater amount."

The retailer buys the seller's property with the loan on the new building, plus a loan secured by the sales proceeds on retailer's existing building. The loan could be provided either by a third party lender, or by the seller using the net proceeds from the sale. The example below will track a potential loan to the retailer by the seller of the new building.

## SUMMARY OF TRANSACTION

### Step 1: Loan on Other Building:

Seller → Lends the retailer $150,000 on the future sales proceeds

Retailer → Gives the seller a first mortgage on the other building

### Step 2: Sale of Seller's Building:

Retailer → Pays the seller $300,000 for the seller's building

Seller → Deeds the new building to the retailer

Lender → Makes a $150,000 loan to the retailer on the new building

Retailer → Gives the lender first mortgage on the retailer's new building

### Step 3: Repayment of Loan:

Retailer → Pays off the $150,000 loan to the seller (upon sale of other building)

Seller → Releases the first mortgage on the retailer's other building

## BENEFITS

### Benefits to Seller:

The seller sells a building that has been difficult to sell to a qualified buyer *now* rather than later.

The seller also sells the property at full (not discounted) price because of the benefit of the loan made by the seller to the retailer.

The seller eliminates any risk due to insurance coverage issues on a vacant building.

The seller is relieved of liability on a $150,000 bank loan.

The seller also gets cash in six months upon the sale of the other property.

**Benefits to Retailer:**

The retailer gets to move in now and take advantage of the new location for the holiday season business.

The retailer gets to use their expected sales proceeds now rather than later.

The retailer gets the opportunity for a new banking relationship with the bank, which is providing the assumption of the existing loan on the new building.

**Possible Risks:**

If the retailer is not able to close the sale of their other building for any reason, the seller may not get paid on the equity at the end of the Christmas season. The seller may have to wait for some additional time. The seller might even have to take title to the retailer's free and clear building. However, consider that still may be an acceptable "step up" for the seller. The seller has sold a difficult building for full price, been relieved of $150,000 liability on the bank loan, and now owns a first mortgage on a property that the neighbor is interested in buying.

The retailer may end up with two loans and two payments if his sale does not close for any reason. Again, that still may be an acceptable situation given the expected increase in retail business at the new location. The company must balance the benefits against the total of the costs and the risks.

Both the seller and the retailer can approximately determine the risks of the transaction (as in any transaction) by using the principle of getting all of the facts.

## KEY POINTS

This "loan on future sales proceeds" strategy allows potential buyers to acquire property *now* using the contract of sale they have on other property. They do not need to wait until that sale is closed *later* to buy a property *now*!

Similar to any transaction involving making a loan to a private party, you will want to employ the appropriate legal counsel. Again, a third-party loan facilitator may be advisable, especially where you are making a loan secured by property in another state.

A major caveat is that there is never a guarantee of a consummated sale on the other property the buyer is financing. Many contracts fail between the contract stage and the final closing stage. If you are the one making the loan, be prepared for possible issues in that closing. You may have that loan in place for longer than you expect. Include these other possible outcomes in your decision-making criteria.

# LEASE WITH AN OPTION OR CONTRACT TO PURCHASE

## STRATEGY

There are many variations of creative seller financing. A lease with an option or contract to purchase is really seller financing without any down payment.

A buyer does not always need to own a property in order to gain from some of the benefits of ownership. Sometimes a buyer can control a property through other approaches. Likewise, a seller does not always have to sell a property immediately to be free of some of the obligations of ownership. Sometimes, a seller can accomplish some of these goals in other ways.

One example of another way is a lease with an option to purchase. In a lease with an option to purchase, a tenant (buyer) makes monthly lease payments over some period of time. All or portions of those lease payments may even apply to the purchase of the property. The lease and the monthly payments are an incentive to the seller to grant the tenant (buyer) an option to purchase sometime during or at the end of the lease period.

A buyer and seller could also accomplish a similar with a lease with a *contract* to purchase, where the tenant commits to the purchase of a property at the time of the execution of the lease. A *remodeling* agreement with an option or a contract to purchase could also be used where the remodeler commits to a closing date on the purchase that is after completion of the remodeling. A buyer could also use a contract to pur-

CREATIVE SELLING FINANCING

chase with *monthly earnest money and a long closing period*. Each of these are variations on the same theme of the seller transferring control of a property before the actual closing in order to gain some other benefit.

Furthermore, there are numerous possibilities beyond these. The form of the transaction is less important here than the overall concept. You can create endless variations on this theme.

Examples of the lease with an option or contract to purchase approach are shown below.

## RESIDENTIAL EXAMPLE

Imagine that you have found a house you want to buy. The property is attractive and in good condition, but it is located in a neighborhood with a large number of similar properties for sale. Sales in the area are currently weak, but there is a strong rental demand. Furthermore, you believe that demand for houses in the area will increase over time.

The sellers have put the house on the market as they are planning to relocate to a new city in a few months.

Assume that your buy/no buy standard for a purchase to buy, spruce up, and resell is 70% of market value. You have established that threshold based upon your perceived risk in the current marketplace. It also in-cludes the amount of cost and time required to be in a position to close a resale.

NOTE: Your threshold or formula for deciding whether it is a good deal for you is completely an individual decision. There is no magic number!

Your negotiations with the homeowner are stalled with their sticking to a price that is equal to 85% of Market Value. They are firm on their desired purchase price, as they do not need to sell right away. They are planning to rent a home in the new city they are moving to before making a decision to purchase. It is clear to you that, while they want to have cash from a sale, they do not have to have cash in order to move into another house.

Given the seller's firmness on price, do you pass and go onto another deal?

You certainly could pass, but you do have a lot of time invested in your research and negotiations to this point. How might you still be able to purchase the property, make a profit, and not compromise your buy/no buy standard for a flip?

## SOLUTION

You could negotiate a purchase contract tied to a twelve-month lease. You want to perform the same level of due diligence on the lease market as you do on the sales market. After all, you are making a sizeable commitment for your lease (and expected sublease) as you are for your purchase. A thorough examination of the property, as well as the "for sale" market and "for rent" market, is warranted.

The lease should include the right to sublease to another person. You would be obligated to close the purchase at the end of twelve months. You could have the start date of the lease and the twelve-month period to purchase the property both begin on the date the seller's move (but after your due diligence is complete).

As a buyer, you might want to have your attorney create a recordable "Memorandum of Equitable Interest" or similar recordable document setting forth that you have a contract to purchase the property. This would prevent the owners from selling the property to someone else before your transaction closes.

You now have the time to look for a buyer. You now could sublease the property to another person, which would allow you to gain the monthly cash flow during the lease-option period. You could lease to a tenant with a contract to purchase requiring them to close on the purchase in nine months. You could use any one of many different variations on this theme to make a profit.

Assuming that you have verified the decision with the proper due diligence, you may be able to afford the higher purchase price because of the time you have negotiated to finalize your purchase. To do this without a significant amount of risk, you will want to have a realistic strategy to sublease the property quickly and then later to buy the property and quickly resell it.

## Summary of Transaction

### Step 1: Sign Purchase Contract, Lease, and Memorandum

Buyer → Contracts to buy the house at a price equal to 85 percent of the market value

Buyer → Leases the house for twelve months with the right to sublease the house

Buyer → Records a "Memorandum of Equitable Interest" at the county courthouse

### Step 2: Sublease House to the Cover Holding Costs on the Lease

Buyer → Uses the due diligence period to locate a tenant

Buyer → Subleases the house to a tenant for twelve months

### Step 3: House Purchase and Resale with Option to Purchase

Buyer → Locates a buyer for the house during the twelve-month lease period (this could be the tenant to whom you leased the property)

Buyer → Closes on the purchase of the house under a purchase contract

Buyer → Simultaneously closes on the resale of the house at a higher price

## BENEFITS

**Benefits to Sellers:**

The sellers receive a contract of sale at an acceptable price.

The sellers get time to find and close on a new house.

The sellers receive peace of mind.

**Benefits to Buyer:**

The buyer has time to find a renter/buyer with a reduced risk.

## COMMERCIAL OR INVESTMENT EXAMPLE NO. 1

I wanted to buy a large hotel in Dallas. I believed that it was a good candidate to remodel and increase the value of the hotel through good management and marketing. However, I did not have the substantial equity required to purchase the property.

### SOLUTION

I wrote a contract for a newly formed Limited Liability Corporation (LLC) to buy the property *subject to* the LLC obtaining sufficient financing for the purchase. The LLC would also be the operating entity for the hotel.

Once the property was under contract, I arranged for an investment group to put up 100 percent of the money and take title to the property. At the closing of the purchase, my LLC executed a long-term lease for the hotel. Because of the financial strength of the partners and the long-term lease, the investment group secured a long-term loan with a local bank for an amount equal to 75 percent purchase price. The partners of the investment group invested the rest of the cash from a sale of another property that they jointly owned.

Simultaneous with the execution of the long-term lease, the investment group also granted a long-term option to my LLC to purchase the hotel based upon a pre-determined formula. We began operating the hotel beginning on the date of the closing of the hotel purchase by the investment group and the execution of the lease and option with the LLC.

At a later point, my LLC purchased the hotel under the option and then resold it to another group with a new long-term lease and a new long-term option to purchase.

## SUMMARY OF TRANSACTION:

### Step 1: Sign Purchase Contract and Lease

Operating entity (LLC) → Signs a purchase contract to buy the hotel

Operating entity (LLC) → Assigns the contract to an investment group

Investment group → Closes on the purchase of the hotel

Operating entity (LLC) → Executes a long-term lease of the hotel with an option to purchase

### Step 2: Operation of Hotel to Cover Holding Costs on Lease

Operating entity (LLC) → Operates hotel

### Step 3: Hotel Purchase and Resale with Option to Purchase

Operating entity (LLC) → Closes on the purchase of the hotel via the option to purchase

Operating entity (LLC) → Simultaneously closes on a resale of the hotel at a higher price

New investment group → Closes on the purchase of the hotel at a higher price

Operating entity (LLC) → Executes a new long-term lease with an option to purchase

Operating entity (LLC) → Records a new lease with an option to purchase recorded of record at the county courthouse

## BENEFITS

### Benefits to Operating Entity (LLC)

Operating entity (LLC) → Controlled the property long-term with no equity investment.

Operating entity (LLC) → Received an option to purchase at a predetermined price

### Benefits to Investment Group

Investment group → Obtained a favorable loan to purchase price

Investment group → Got a monthly lease payment and good return on equity investment

Investment group → Obtained investment with no management responsibility

### Benefits to Investment Group No. 2

Investment group No. 2 → Obtained a favorable loan to purchase price

Investment group No. 2 → Got a monthly lease payment and good return on equity investment

Investment group No. 2 → Obtained investment with no management responsibility

### Commercial or Investment Example No. 2

To demonstrate one of the many variations on this strategy, John Brennan, CCIM, of Dallas adds his example:

"In 2013, we closed a lease/purchase transaction for a buyer on an apartment complex in Wichita, Kansas.

Seller owned approximately 55 units valued at $1,800,000 with approximately $1,400,000 of debt that was coming due in less than one year.

The buyer felt that he might not yet qualify for a new mortgage at the time of the proposed sale.

The seller was not interested in providing seller financing, yet was highly motivated to eliminate the day-to-day management of the units from her life.

Buyer and seller both executed a master lease of the property with a term of three years.

The buyer took over complete responsibility of the management of the units, collected all of the rents, and paid all bills, including debt service and property taxes. The master lease further provided that the buyer had the right to buy the property at $1,800,000 during the three-year term.

The seller refinanced the property prior to recording the master lease of record in the county courthouse. The buyer paid $400,000 option consideration to the seller that became nonrefundable after the expiration of the inspection period specified in the master lease."

## SUMMARY OF TRANSACTION

### Step 1: Lease with Option

Seller → Borrows additional money secured by mortgage on property

Buyer → Executes three-year master lease with option to purchase at $1,800,000 purchase price

Buyer → Gives seller $400,000 option consideration

Buyer → Records master lease with option to purchase in public record

Seller → Gives buyer three-year option to purchase at $1,800,000 price

## Step 2: Exercise of Option to Purchase (In the Future)

Buyer → Pays $1,400,000 to seller ($1,800,000 purchase price minus $400,000 option consideration)

Seller → Pays off existing underlying loans

Seller → Gives buyer deed to property free and clear of all debt

## Benefits to Seller

The seller had no more management responsibility through the master lease.

The seller received a substantial option fee, which was not taxable to the seller until the buyer exercises purchase option.

The seller received the entire purchase price in cash at the end of the three year lease.

## Benefits to Buyer

The buyer was able to take over complete operations of property.

The buyer had a set purchase price to buy the units over three years.

The buyer now had the time to qualify for a new loan or loan assumption prior to the exercise of the purchase.

## KEY POINTS

A lease/option strategy provides the buyer the time to close the transaction without significant cash investment at the outset. The lease should contain the right to sublease the property to generate cash flow until the time comes to close on the purchase of the property.

A lease with a contract to purchase, or a remodeling agreement with an option or contract to purchase, or even a contract to purchase with monthly earnest money and a long closing period can be used to accomplish the same result.

The buyer receiving the option would be wise to record the lease with an option to purchase (if the option is contained in the lease), or a memorandum of equitable interest if the option is a document separate from the lease, in order to protect their option to purchase. Otherwise, any lien against the property or the seller that is recorded between the time the option is executed and the closing on the purchase could affect the buyer's rights to exercise that option. I advise you to consult an attorney about how to handle this in your jurisdiction.

# CONCLUSION

It is obvious that the potential variety of these creative seller financing transactions is endless. Every situation is different. The other party to the transaction is always unique. The properties are never the same. You are also constantly changing in your needs and desired benefits.

When you are negotiating a transaction, ask yourself the following question: "How can creative seller financing create added benefits in this transaction?" By answering the question newly in each transaction, you will find new and unique ways to use the tool.

Remember that creative seller financing is still only a tool. Just as a master artisan uses the right tool for the right job, use this tool where appropriate. Do not try to force it if the tool is ineffective.

There are also many traditional financing tools that you will find are more appropriate for a given situation. Creative seller financing is still only one of the many tools in the world of creative real estate. I would be happy to provide you more ideals and tools in my Creative Real Estate Book Series.

Put the ideas in this book and our other books *into action and gain practice* in using these tools in your own life, and in your own transactions.

# THANK YOU!

I hope you have enjoyed this, the first book in the *Creative Real Estate Book Series*. It is my intention that you are equipped with more answers to close more real estate deals!

Check out our second book titled *Creative Down Payments* on Amazon. com. I would also appreciate it very much if you could leave a short comment on Amazon.

Also, I invite you to check out the Creative Real Estate Network web site at CreativeRealEstateNetwork.com.

Many thanks!

*Chuck Sutherland*

# GLOSSARY

**Add Value** - An amount added to the value of a product or service through entrepreneurship

**All-Inclusive Deed of Trust** - A Deed of Trust, which encompasses and includes all other Deeds of Trust that have a superior priority

**All-Inclusive Wrap-Around Mortgage** - A Mortgage, which encompasses and includes all other mortgages that have a superior priority

**Amortized** - A loan with regular payments at an interval over a specific period of time, which completely pays off the principal and interest during that period

**As Remodeled Value** - The value of a property after repairs and improvements

**Asking Price** - The price at which a parcel of real estate is offered for sale

**Assumption** - Taking on another's responsibilities or financial obligation (such as a loan)

**Balloon** - Loan installment or other payment (paid usually at the end of the loan period) to substantially reduce or pay off a loan

**Benefit** - An advantage or profit gained from something

**Boots on the Ground** - Usually denotes a person who physically conducts or oversees the performance of some action

**Capitalization Rate** - The rate of return on a real estate investment property based on the expected income that the property (see Yield)

**Carrying Costs** - The costs associated with owning a parcel of real estate

**Closing** - The completion of a transaction involving the sale or exchange or real estate

**Closing Agent** - An individual company that handles the closing of a parcel of real property and the legal transfer of title and ownership from the seller to the buyer

**Collateral Security** - Property pledged by a borrower to protect the interests of the lender

**Consumer Credit** - Credit extended to individuals for personal or household use, rather than businesses

**Conventional Financing** - A loan that conforms to conditions and terms of the general financing marketplace. Sometimes refers to a loan other than one guaranteed by the Veterans Administration or insured by the federal housing administration

**Creative Financing** - Financing that is "outside the box" of traditional real estate financing

**Creditor** - A person or entity to whom a debt is owed

**Curb Appeal** - The visual attractiveness of a property as viewed from the street

**Deal** - A financial transaction

**Deed of Trust** - In real estate, a deed of trust is a deed to real property that is transferred to a trustee that holds it as security for a loan (debt) between a borrower and lender

**Detriment** - A disadvantage or loss from something

**Developer** - A person or company that builds and sells houses or other buildings on a piece of land

**Dodd-Frank Act** - The "Dodd-Frank Wall Street Reform and Consumer Protection Act." A compendium of federal regulations, primarily affecting financial institutions and their customers Passed in 2010 and effective in January 2014

**Down Payment** - A part of the full purchase price paid at the time of purchase with the balance to from the proceeds of a loan

**Due Diligence** - The process of investigating and researching a property or situation to determine actual or potential risks

**Duplex** - A two-unit property where the units normally attached

**Equity** - The net value of a property after any debts and other obligations have been subtracted

**Escrow** - Money, deed, or some other asset held in trust by a third party to be turned over to the receiving party only upon fulfillment of one or more conditions

**Escrow Account** - A special account for holding specific monies for disbursement under specific conditions

**Escrow Closing** - The process of selling or buying a property where an independent third party holds and disburses all documents and money upon completion of the conditions of the closing.

**Existing Financing** - The current secured by a property and/or a guarantee

**First Deed of Trust** - A Deed of Trust first in priority before other Deeds of Trust

**First Mortgage** - A Mortgage first in priority before other Mortgages

**Fix and Flip** - To buy and usually renovate (real estate) so as to quickly resell at a higher price

**Flip** - To buy and usually resell property so as to quickly resell at a higher price

**Free and Clear** - Free from any debt or encumbrance

**Guarantee** - A promise for the fulfillment of something

**Lease with a Contract to Purchase (a/k/a Lease Purchase)** - A Lease of property for a specified time with an agreement to buy that property on or before a specified date

**Lease with an Option to Purchase** - A Lease of property for a specified time with an option by the Buyer to buy that property on or before a specified date

**Loan Facilitator** - An individual or company that manages the loan process in a closing of the purchase of property

**Loan to Value (a/k/a "LTV")** - The amount of money borrowed in relation to the total market value of a property

**LTV** - See Loan to Value

**Market Value** - The most probable price that a property would bring in a competitive and open market under fair sale conditions

**Market Value Appraisal** - A professional opinion, usually written, of the market value of a property, such as a home, business, or other asset

**Market Yield** - The annual return of an investment divided by the market value

**MLO** - See Mortgage Loan Originators

**Mortgage** - A conveyance of or lien against property (as for securing a loan) that becomes void upon payment or performance according to stipulated terms

**Mortgage Loan Originators (a/k/a "MLOs")** - An individual or company that originates a mortgage in a real estate transaction

**Mortgagee** - The lender in a mortgage loan transaction

**Mortgagor** - The borrower in a mortgage loan transaction

**Must-Have** - In real estate, something that is essential to have or obtain by a party to the transaction

**Nationwide Mortgage Licensing System & Registry (a/k/a "NMLS")** - A national registry of Mortgage Loan Originators (a/k/a MLOs)

**Net Benefits** - The advantage or profit gained from something after consideration of the disadvantages and costs

**Net Operating Income (a/k/a NOI)** - The total of all sources of income, less vacancy, credit losses, and operating expenses

**NMLS** - See Nationwide Mortgage Licensing System & Registry

**NOI** - See Net Operating Income

**Note** - A written promise to pay a debt under specific terms and conditions

**Opportunity Cost** - The cost of using a resource to acquire one thing instead of another

**Option** - In real estate, a right to buy or sell something for a specified price during a specified period

**Owner Value** - The value that an owner of property places on that property

**Ownership Costs** - In real estate, the costs of owning a certain property which include loan payments, taxes, maintenance, and management

**Party or Parties** - A person or entity that is involved in a legal case or contract

**Potential Market Value** - The estimated price that a property would bring in a competitive and open market under fair sale conditions and under some assumptions as to how the property can be improved under a particular plan

**Potential Net Operating Income** - The estimated total of all sources of income, less vacancy, credit losses, and operating expenses under some assumptions as to how the property can be improved under a particular plan

**Qualify (for a loan)** - To meet the requirements or conditions to receive or assume a loan

**Realtor** - A member of the National Association of Realtors

**Relocation Company** - A firm that arrange the relocation of the employees of a company or entity from one city to another

**Remodeled Market Value** - The estimated price that a property would bring in a competitive and open market under fair sale conditions and under some assumptions as to how the property can be remodeled under a particular plan

**Remodeler** - A person or company that remodels and improves real property

**Remodeling Agreement** - The agreement between the owner of a property and a person or company that remodels and improves real property

**Return on Investment (a/k/a ROI)** - The results of an action compared to the costs. In real estate, the term refers to the percentage expressed by the financial yield divided by the cost of the investment

**ROI** - See Return on Investment

**SAFE Act** - The "Secure and Fair Enforcement for Mortgage Licensing Act of 2008"

**Second Deed of Trust** - A Deed of Trust second in priority behind another Deed of Trust

**Second Mortgage** - A Mortgage second in priority behind another Mortgage

**Security** - Something given as a pledge for the fulfillment of some obligation

**Seller Financing** - The Seller of a property making a loan for a Buyer to purchase the Seller's property

**Subject To** - Conditional or dependent on something

**Subordinated** - A debt or obligation that has a lower priority in repayment than some other debt or obligation

**Sweat Equity** - The value or results from the work that a person does to improve something

**Third Deed of Trust** - A Deed of Trust third in priority behind two other Deeds of Trust

**Third Mortgage** - A Mortgage third in priority behind two other Mortgages

**Third-Party Lender** - An independent lender not associated with the Buyer or Seller

**Title Company** - A company in the business of examining title to real estate and issuing title insurance Title companies often hold the earnest money from a contract to sell real property and manage the closing process

**Turn Around** - The process of improving a poorly producing property through investment and management

**Underwriting** - The process during which lenders analyze the risks a particular borrower presents and either declines to make the loan or sets appropriate conditions for the loan

**Value** - The amount of money that something is worth

**Wholesale Buyer** - In real estate, an individual or company that buys property at a substantial discount below the estimated market value

**Yield** - The financial return of an investment, usually as expressed as the net income divided by the amount of the total investment

CPSIA information can be obtained
at www.ICGtesting.com
Printed in the USA
LVOW10s0040161117
556496LV00001B/43/P